THROUGH THE
GLASS CEILING

THROUGH THE GLASS CEILING

Reflections on Feminism from the C-Suite

SHEELAGH WHITTAKER

 Sutherland House Experts

TORONTO, 2025

Sutherland House Experts Corporation
260 Heath Street West
Suite 605
Toronto, Ontario
M5P 3L6

Copyright © 2025 by Sheelagh Whittaker

All rights reserved, including the right to reproduce this book or portions thereof in any form whatsoever. For information on rights and permissions or to request a special discount for bulk purchases, please contact Sutherland House Experts at info@sutherlandhouseexperts.com

Sutherland House Experts and logo are registered trademarks.

First edition, March 2025

Manufactured in Turkey
Cover designed by Jordan Lunn
Book composed by Karl Hunt

Library and Archives Canada Cataloguing in Publication
Title: Through the glass ceiling : reflections on feminism from the C-suite / Sheelagh Whittaker.
Names: Whittaker, M. Sheelagh, author
Identifiers: Canadiana (print) 2024051484X | Canadiana (ebook) 20240514874 |
ISBN 9781738396481 (softcover) | ISBN 9781738396498 (EPUB)
Subjects: LCSH: Whittaker, M. Sheelagh. | LCSH: Feminism. | LCSH: Leadership in women. | LCSH: Successful women.
Classification: LCC HQ1155 .W45 2025 | DDC 305.42—dc23

ISBN 978-1-7383964-8-1
eBook 978-1-7383964-9-8

Contents

*Prologues (Yes, plural): A Potted History of the
"Glass Ceiling"* ix
*Through the Glass Ceiling: Reflections on Feminism from
the C-Suite* xiii

Chapter 1: Rising to Trudy-Ann's Challenge 1

Chapter 2: Developing the Right Stuff 5

Chapter 3: Filling the Behavioral Development Interstices ... 9

Chapter 4: The Best Role Model Ever 15

Chapter 5: Aspiration Defined 19

Chapter 6: The Theatre of the Absurd as a Touchstone ... 21

Chapter 7: Finally, Feminism Penetrates My Consciousness ... 24

Chapter 8: Things I Did in Business School (not all of them, of course) ... 29

Chapter 9: Things I Learned in Business School 35

Chapter 10: The Singular of Premises Is Not "Premise" ... 37

Chapter 11: A Feminist Family Anthem 44

Chapter 12: Keep Trying until You Get It Right 46

Chapter 13: A Swift One to the Ankle 52

Chapter 14: Evolving 57

Chapter 15: The Kids Are All Right — 63

Chapter 16: The Days Mommy Got Angry — 65

Chapter 17: Being a Witness Seems to Run in the Family — 68

Chapter 18: Proceeding along as a Non-Linear Thinker — 78

Chapter 19: Beaming Up — 81

Chapter 20: Games Your Mother Couldn't Teach You — 83

Chapter 21: Never a Dull Moment — 91

Chapter 22: Walking in the Footprints of Ross Perot — 95

Chapter 23: November 6, 1993: Who Should Be Nervous? — 99

Chapter 24: Back at the Ranch — 102

Chapter 25: A Stranger in a Strange Land — 106

Chapter 26: Big Corporations Have Their Own Social Norms — 108

Chapter 27: The Times (and the Locations) They Are a-Changin . . . — 111

Chapter 28: Horizontal Emigration — 118

Chapter 29: "A Female Leader? And a Colonial at That?" — 124

Chapter 30: It Turns Out You *Can* Break a Glass Ceiling Feet First — 127

Chapter 31: "I Ain't Down Yet" — 130

Chapter 32: Evolution Makes Up 89% of the Word "Revolution" — 133

Chapter 33: Varying My Shots — 135

Chapter 34: I Rise Again — 137

Chapter 35: And So It Goes, and So It Goes . . . — 141

Chapter 36: Important Lesson for Me: Second-Wave Feminism Has Had Its Day — 143

Acknowledgments — 149

*To my beloved sister Penny—when you
read this book you will know why.*

PROLOGUES (YES, PLURAL)

A Potted History of the "Glass Ceiling"

WHEN I WAS growing up in Western Canada in the early 1960s, middle-class girls' aspirations were generally directed toward the role of the well-educated wife and mother, possibly augmented by a brief early job in retail to contribute education funds for her husband or to provide a little start-up money for the family. When I moved on to the aspirations-embracing stage of life, the Western world was hatching the idea that working women might be allowed a slightly larger role in the workplace. It had worked pretty well during the Second World War, so maybe it was worth a peacetime kick at a small can, not at making a dent in any glass ceiling.

After the revelation unfolded that the kick in fact boosted GDP and national productivity, policymakers and public intellectuals alike realized that working women could get pregnant (at least the married ones). First maternity leave and then *paid* maternity leave were at issue, and, by 1971, Unemployment Insurance benefits in Canada were modified to include fifteen weeks of paid maternity leave.

Paid maternity leave was advertised by the federal government as covering 67 percent of a woman's salary for fifteen weeks. What they didn't mention was that there was an annual earnings ceiling caveat, after which the government's contribution was proportionately taxed back. I forget the numbers, but I remember that in my case, as a "Combines Officer 2," my net take-home number for paid maternity leave was ridiculously low. So: I saved up my annual leave for my maternity leave.

In those days (the late 1970s) the route to authority, high pay, and languorous lunches in both business and the civil service was painted in metaphor. This took the form of a ladder with many rungs where only the strong and the mighty (men) made it to the top. Then suddenly, or so it seemed, there was vague talk about women being allowed to climb onto the lower rungs of the ladder to success. One problem with that imagery is that it was hard to figure out how precisely to move from rung to rung.

The increased scrutiny on genuine upward mobility for women, fueled by the feminist movement of the late 1960s and 1970s, revealed a lot of flaws in the ladder metaphor, including difficulties portraying the number of rungs, the stability of the rungs, whether you stood on them or clung to the rung above, and how much space there was on the uppermost rung, not to mention the lack of clarity about what was so alluring up there at the top and, most of all, what the ladder was leaning on.

In 1978, at a "Woman's Exposition" in New York City, a quick-witted young American female consultant, Marilyn Loden, first conceived of the metaphor of a glass ceiling with the area below it occupied by working women facing unequal pay, a lack of role models, and an absence of champions, while the area above these female denizens was reserved for those, predominantly male, who had achieved status and money and security in their employment.

The glass ceiling metaphor caught on. Others took credit for it. It appeared "officially" in the press for the first time in *AdWeek* in 1984. The notion of women being able to see that there was more to gain above you but you couldn't access it because it was protected by a thick, intransigent barrier captured the feminist zeitgeist of the times.

The image also resonated since it made sense. You can break glass but it isn't easy. Journalists found it a simple and evocative image to use. Good shorthand for a complex and dynamic and ubiquitous problem, the stifling of women in business who were caught working busily, but in a trap, with men looking down on them.

Feminists with a platform, and the broader communications media, also embraced the notion of a glass ceiling as useful shorthand for the nearly institutionalized resistance toward giving women executive roles in the workplace. It was a step toward solving the problem by describing it.

I must admit, I did spend some time trying to visualize a metaphoric elevator to the top floor.

My files are not organized in the manner in which they might have been when I was a CEO, but as I was looking through them recently, one newspaper headline jumped out, possibly because of the mixed metaphor:

> "Stuck on the Ladder—Not only is the glass ceiling still in place, but men and women have very different views of the problem." (*Maclean's*, October 20, 1997)

Yeah, right, I thought. It was a point-of-view exercise. Even in the late 1990s, women were still being envisioned as looking up at the soles of shoes and pant cuffs while the men were looking at each other. ("Hey Joe—golf tomorrow?") Occasionally, a shard of glass involuntarily broke off from under the floor and fell on a woman going by. If it didn't injure her, it gave her hope.

These days the phrase "glass ceiling" is considered to be rather "old hat." (Is that a mixed metaphor?) Society has moved on to more colorful issues like LGBTQ+ rights. But my present advice to women still stems from those heady days of Women's Lib. As originated by my friend Bobbie at our Women's Group at the University of Guelph in 1972,

> "Ladies—we need to pull ourselves up by the hair on our legs."

Knowledge, after all, is information refined by experience, sound judgment, and care.

Through the Glass Ceiling: Reflections on Feminism from the C-Suite

THIS BOOK ISN'T just about a woman, or just a book for women. This book is about a person—me, Sheelagh Whittaker. A person who turned out to be lucky, lucky, lucky and has had the good sense to realize it.

But things didn't start out that way. I started out simply wanting to be more than I was, to leap tall buildings and meet interesting people, wanting to be loved and admired. And I kept on trying.

This book is about how, at a critical time in my development, I realized that life can be challenging and fun and that my gender was just a fact, not a handicap. That realization coincided with a time when women went looking for ways to change their perspectives. They went looking to play a new role in society. And that timing was a big part of my luck.

And now I realize, as I've written it, that all the experimenting and questing has made men freer to be whimsical and experimental too, to go with their notions and their dreams and confess stuff—and avoid shoveling the snow. So give this a try, guys. Think of yourself as the "any man" starting off with a partially mapped life and see what new territories you stumble into and what the stumbling inspires within you.

Some years ago, when I imagined that the hurly-burly of my career was almost done, I wrote a vaguely autobiographical book. My heroine, called

Evaline, was an almost irrepressible product of the theory and practice of feminism. There is a scene where Evaline receives a phone call from a BBC executive, asking to set up a radio interview to discuss feminism and the rise of women closing the pay gap.

Here's a brief excerpt from that book, which was entitled *Evaline, A Feminist's Tale*.

* * *

Bearing Witness

"I am here today in the BBC studio with Ms. Evaline Sadlier, a self-described feminist and businesswoman whose career has spanned the Atlantic. Can I call you Evaline?"

"Please do. And what should I call you?"

"Oh. Please call me David . . . Much-lauded businesswoman, consultant, non-executive board member, proud mother and grandmother. It sounds like you are a real Superwoman."

"Absolutely not."

"Tell us, then, how would you describe yourself?"

"I am a very lucky woman, a woman who has had the chance to live the life she wanted."

"So you didn't need quotas or rules or burning bras to help you get along."

"Of course I did. I needed every bit of help I could get. I needed role models and encouragement and legislation and awareness-raising and support from many women and men along the way. I needed every bit of it."

"And is the job done? Are the goals of feminism achieved?"

"Again, absolutely not. We are a long way from gender equality even in the developed world, much less the parts of the world where women are still treated like slaves or chattels. Feminism is about natural justice and we still have a long way to go."

"But, as you said, you personally have lived the life you wanted. Any regrets?"

(Dead air . . . dead air . . . dead air . . .)

"No. No, regrets."

"None at all?"

"Well, of course, every life has its highs and lows. I have suffered some painful losses. And I have done some things that I wish I hadn't done: laughed at indiscreet moments, sung off-key in the business voice choir, kissed some frogs who turned out to be toads, failed to properly understand the tears of a child—but who hasn't? I am the sum of all my mistakes as well as all my triumphs."

"So that's it?"

"Yes, that's about it."

* * *

But life didn't imitate art. And that radio interview (a version of which really happened) was not the summation of a fulfilling career. Not only was it not "about it," it wasn't even the beginning of the end, although it may have been the end of the beginning.

Much later, at the age of seventy-five, after a devastating interval where I lost first my son, Daniel, then my husband, William, not to mention enduring a back operation for an exotic condition called *cauda equina* (Latin for "horse's tail" on account of its appearance) and a dose of COVID-fueled alienation, along came Trudy-Ann, my Caribbean practical nurse, carer, and straight talker. Trudy was not prepared to accept lassitude from me just because I was engaged in a miracle recovery from a very tricky surgery after a period of heartbreaking losses. No, Trudy made me walk around our building, clinging to large palm trees as I moaned in agony, and all throughout she made me think about this book, the one you're presently reading.

"You've got all this stuff to tell us about what you've done and what you are going to do next," she encouraged. "So do it."

Trudy even bought me a notebook so I could record my scattered thoughts.

So, Trudy, here it goes.

CHAPTER ONE

Rising to Trudy-Ann's Challenge

MY FIRST THOUGHT was to try to place myself in context. These days, increasingly, there are those who think of feminism as twentieth century or old hat. Some years ago, I went to chair a debate at the University of Toronto's Hart House with a distinct female advancement slant and realized that much of my revolutionary syllabus was outdated, that I was becoming a relic, left behind like a pedant correcting people when they made the mistake of saying "man hours" instead of "work hours" or "staff hours" around me while women were becoming university presidents.

Of course, feminism is a continuum, and I am a living witness from the days when *Playgirl* was a novelty. (The inaugural issue in June 1973 featured TV star Lyle Waggoner as the naked centerfold. It was a wonderful and clever way of demonstrating role reversal.) But I did live it, "feminism in full," and now I can reflect about our successes and our failures and our right to be as admirable or obnoxious as the next person. Like that famous line in the battle cry: "I am woman." "Yes, I've paid the price, but look how much I've gained!"

But this isn't supposed to just be about me. There are those who came before and those who are coming afterward.

Nowadays, we categorize generations using labels like the Greatest Generation, the Silent Generation, Baby Boomers, Generation X, Millennials, and now Generation Z (or Gen Zed, as I call it). My colleagues, friends, and close relatives belong to one or more of these generational cohorts. Throughout this treatise exploring the experiences of growing up female, I will intersperse comments and perspectives from them to provide insights across the generational spectrum.

I start with the words of my good friend Merrijoy Kelner, who has become my role model, even though I didn't meet her until four years ago, when she was ninety-two.

A Representative of the Greatest Generation

By Merrijoy Kelner, PhD

My first feminist thoughts were individual, not societal.

It was the early sixties, and I was feeling unsatisfied and restless. I had married in 1949, at the age of 21. That was an era when women were expected to marry, raise a family, and support their husband's careers. For a time, that limited picture suited me; I thought it was the way I was supposed to live my life. After a while, however, the constraints began to chafe. By the time I reached my thirties, I began to wonder if there were other possibilities out there for me. Although feminism was just developing as a social movement, I was concentrating on my own discontents.

I had always been a good student, and eventually I decided to go back to university to pursue a graduate degree. My husband was appalled. I told him about my plans when we were dining in a famous restaurant. There were singing waiters, a welcoming ambience and good food. It seemed an opportune time to broach the subject. He responded: "How can you think of such a thing? Your children need you and I need you."

I tried to explain that I required more stimulation and purpose in my life, but he was adamant. So I told him: "Either I go back to school, or I take lovers. I need more in my life." Eventually I prevailed and enrolled as a graduate student at the University of Toronto. I did well in my studies and continued on to complete a PhD.

It was around this time that I became aware of the feminist movement. It reinforced my determination to develop my own identity. Slowly I began to think of myself as a scholar and that view was encouraged by my professors.

One day, the head of the department asked me to come to his office. He was my thesis supervisor, so I attached no particular importance to the invitation. But when he offered me a cup of coffee, something he had never done before, I sensed that this meeting was different. Then he told me that the professor who taught the course on "Power and Social Status" was going on sabbatical the next year. He asked if I felt capable of teaching the course.

I had been studying those concepts in order to write my thesis on "Ethnic Penetration into the Elite Structure of Toronto." So I answered immediately.

"Yes, I know I can do it."

He responded: "That's settled then. We can pay you seven thousand dollars for the course."

I had recently learned that a fellow student had been offered nine thousand dollars to teach another course in the department. "Why the discrepancy?" I said, "I know that my colleague Allan has been offered more money. Do you think I will do a lesser job than he will?" "No," he answered, "But you are a married woman, and you don't need the money." I wanted that job so badly I could taste it. I don't know where I found the courage, but I told him that I couldn't accept unless I was paid the same as my male colleague. Finally, he acceded, and I was paid nine thousand dollars for teaching the course.

I must have done a good job, because next term I was asked to join the faculty as a lecturer, and I was on my way to a career in academia.

Merrijoy had gumption, meaning courage and a go-get-it attitude bundled together. And she still does have gumption. Her latest claim to fame was surviving a ferocious attack from a raccoon with distemper. She has what writer Tom Wolfe first identified as "the right stuff."

CHAPTER TWO

Developing the Right Stuff

DURING MY CAREER, sometimes politely and sometimes rather rudely, I would be asked questions like, "How did you get that job?" or "Aren't you uncomfortable managing all those people?" And once I was introduced as "This is Sheelagh Whittaker and I don't know why she's here," despite my having been the head of the consulting team that successfully won the project. It was hard not to be defensive, but, over time, I began to answer such questions with something glib like "Oh, I don't know. Maybe there was no one else to promote" or "I guess I was a bit haphazardly socialized and don't know when to feel uncomfortable."

No one ever asked me what I meant by "haphazardly socialized" (usually they were too distracted by my unwarranted prize or appointment), but I became increasingly curious as to why my subconscious had come up with that difficult-to-refute answer.

Armed with Sociology 101 from my undergraduate days at the University of Alberta, and assisted by a background study prepared for the Royal Commission on the Status of Women in Canada (1970), I have tried to piece together the nature versus nurture elements of my personal brand of socialization that left me so open to manifesting the tenets of feminism.

For example, on the "nature" side, it is quite clear that I had come by my irreverent exuberance, tangential thinking, and tendency to laugh excessively on account of my genes. These behaviors can be irritating, and my brother, John, is oft quoted by family members for his insightful pronouncement on our mutual tendency to irritate and confuse others by laughing in the face of adversity: "Some people just don't like Whittakers."

(Unfortunately, he didn't mention that until after I had decided to keep my maiden name.)

Still, I was puzzled by people's reactions to me, although I put a lot of it down to unthinking, reflexive sexism. But that didn't seem to be answer enough. So, in the way one does when one is struggling for deeper meaning, I tried to organize information about my upbringing relevant to my ultimate marketplace role as "Glass Ceiling Breaker"—also known as the woman with shards in her hair.

I consulted my touchstone document, *The Development of Sex Role Stereotypes in Women*, a feeder research study prepared for the Royal Commission on the Status of Women.

Sadly, I can't find my copy anymore (maybe a disgruntled spouse threw it away) and the Internet has so far resisted my searches. But I don't need my oft-referred-to copy of the background study to be able to sketch out its major findings.

To my recollection, the researchers' findings were that women with weak alignment to contemporary sex or gender roles tended to have one, or even more, of the following backgrounds:

1. They were the daughter of a woman who had been seriously ill or died during their childhood.
2. They were the oldest daughter in a family of exclusively girl children.
3. They were raised in a family where one sibling, frequently female, was seriously ill.

In the first instance, it suggests that the maturing girl was deprived of a traditional example of wife or mother through her mother's absence or illness.

In the second, the implication is that, deprived of a son in whom to inculcate in the ways of man, the eldest daughter proved well positioned to be taught key elements of the male role, at least as defined by family life.

The third instance is more complicated, but I have assumed that the distraction of having to continuously watch over and care for a child who is unwell leaves the mother with insufficient time and attention to pass on the complete syllabus of appropriate wife/mother behavior to her daughters.

I was the child of a mother with multiple sclerosis at a time when treatment consisted of weekly shots of vitamin B12. She became severely incapacitated and died when I was eighteen. In addition, or maybe partly because of our mother's illness, my younger sister suffered from schizophrenia in her late teens. Schizophrenia was then (and still is today to some extent) blamed on bad mothering, so this societal rebuke may have stung my mother, adding insult to her illness.

Even since I first read the sex-role stereotypes study, I have conducted a private study of my own on the successful women I have encountered in the ideas marketplace.

Here's what I have observed: The mother of Theresa May, the second woman prime minister of the United Kingdom, suffered from multiple sclerosis, as did Anne Volant Rowling, the mother of J.K., of Harry Potter fame.

Several of my most senior comrades-in-arms in the working world had mothers who died young or simply "left the building" for reasons of their own.

A longtime friend and very successful realtor, Linda, was the oldest of three daughters, as was Karyn, my closest female colleague at York University business school, now called the Schulich School, and my accomplished first reader and professor of English, Faith.

There was Therese, a clever and idiosyncratic French-Canadian advertising specialist who went on to international fame working at the United Nations, and Trina, a very successful broadcaster—both had sisters suffering from anorexia or schizophrenia.

I realize there is no conclusive research value in these isolated examples, but they do seem to reveal a certain independence of spirit among those I know.

So, what does this diversion into the sociology of sex-role development suggest? To me it suggests that some girls who were left to make up their own idea of what constitutes womanly behavior during the sixties took their cue from the musical *Annie Get Your Gun*, which came out in 1946, perhaps coincidently Boomer Year One.

I particularly like this lyric from the show.

> *Anything you can do,*
> *I can do better.*
> *I can do anything*
> *Better than you.*

However, "you can't get a man with a gun" wasn't bad advice either.

My family liked to listen to musicals.

CHAPTER THREE

Filling the Behavioral Development Interstices

FOLLOWING MY RUDIMENTARY research on how "girls who don't know any better set out to take their equal place in the world," I reviewed my childhood. I began to realize that I was the beneficiary of a rising wave in the development of twentieth-century feminism and had been lucky enough to surf that wave with joy.

At age four, I had two imaginary constant companions: Boy and Guy. The significance of their names didn't occur to me until much, much later. We had a lot of fun together, and my family seemed happy that I had company and enjoyed my retelling of conversations about the opinions and preferences of Boy and Guy over dinner.

I had quite a happy childhood, if you allow for the fact that my mother slid slowly and elegantly from my life under the curse of MS. She had primary progressive multiple sclerosis, and she was diagnosed when I was in grade school.

With my mother ill and my father often off working on capital projects overseas, much of the initial upbringing of my younger sister Terree and me fell to my sister Penny, who is nine years my senior and a prewar baby. During this period my older brother John seems to have been off on a "frolic of his own," as they say in legal circles.

Penny and John were part of the Silent Generation.

"The Silent Generation"

*through the eyes of Penny Bent,
nee Whittaker, LLD*

I was born at the end of the Great Depression and spent my early childhood during the Second World War.

Without the credo of feminism, I still lived a "new woman" life. I had a lot of luck, sometimes just by being in the right place, and I was willing to accept challenges and I stood my ground.

I have been a pioneer in computing, a professional writer, a housewife, and a lawyer. Married for sixty-four years to the same guy, we have three daughters, all brilliant professionals, and an adopted son on a military pension.

What caused my future to deviate from the norm?

In my early world, women ruled. My father went to war before I could remember him. I was raised by women and a retired, loving grandpa.

The Second World War did rattle the concept of "a woman's place is in the home," and government and industry were obliged to realize women's strengths and abilities, as females took over men's jobs in everything from driving buses to building airplanes and government office work.

Faced with a husband overseas, and two small children to look after, Mom got a job at the Boeing aircraft factory on Sea Island, B.C., and rapidly worked her way up to being an "expeditor." She liked going to work and contributing to the family; her only other income was the tiny amount that the Army sent her each month.

The Second World War ended, and life changed. The amazing, much discussed, beloved absent soldier father came home. This man knew nothing about children.

Sister Sheelagh was born in 1947, and Terree four years later. Finally, actual children.

When Sheelagh was a baby, Dad would take me with him on school holidays or weekends to help with survey work on the Fraser River Dykes. He used the transit and I was the rod-and-chain man (person?) holding a marked stick upright for him to sight. It was a summer of "can't you tell if it's straight or not?" and "to the left" and "my left" and "are you sure the chain is tight?" I was eleven and I must have been all right, because he kept taking me.

Then we moved to Edmonton, where my mother was ultimately diagnosed with progressive multiple sclerosis.

By the time I was sixteen, I was trained to tackle any job whether I knew what to do or not and would teach myself if necessary. I had been looking after my two little sisters, who were nine and thirteen years younger than I, and helping Mom. I was out of high school except for one course (the result of switching provinces), so I went to work in my father's engineering company, where I typed specifications on a now antique form of waxed paper which would then be reproduced in a primitive printer. I also did stencil lettering on blueprints. With this skill set, as soon as I was officially out of school, I got a job at the local airport as a teletype operator doing shift work. This was the main communications system running the airport. Point of history: I was on duty when the first jet plane landed in Edmonton.

I was often the only female at the airport on nights, and that is when I first experienced sexual harassment. When I recall that era, I was so amazingly naive that I was saved from worse than the odd grab or kiss because I clearly didn't understand what was going on.

* * *

Then, still before university, I squeezed in a year in London, England, where I was selected as a debutante by some exercise of influence still unknown to me while I worked for Massey Ferguson as receptionist.

At university, I worked as a summer student for *The Edmonton*

Journal and was hired right after graduation by the Government of Alberta, to create a new position of writer for the Department of Welfare. This was an enormous department including everything from child welfare to homeless people. No sub-department knew what any other knew, and I was to write a manual for social workers describing every scenario that could happen and which documents to use. I had permission to look in any files and talk to anyone. Dream job.

IBM had just sold two computers to the Alberta Government, with the sexy names "7070" and "1401." The government's politics required the training of existing staff to operate them. *No job will be lost to a computer!*

A building was being built to house the machines. IBM created an aptitude test designed to select those who would learn about the machine and become the first applications analysts and programmers. I was sent to take the aptitude test by mistake, and got top marks, which created a problem. The first people tested were supposed to be department heads and financial officers.

Two directors did very poorly: the head of the Department of Drivers Licenses, Ralph Crouch, and the head of Motor Vehicles, Dick Ball. We were made into a team. They both knew the existing systems, and I was to create the new one. While this was happening, I got engaged and married and changed my name to Bent. There is no way you could arrange our names that did not sound like a joke, but team Crouch, Ball and Bent (with variations) sat in a small room in temporary rented offices and converted two of the most archaic systems in the province to operational computer applications.

When the Computer Building was finished, the computers delivered, and testing started, I was one of the people who operated the computers. There were few of us, and we worked 12-hour shifts. When everything was operational and running smoothly, I was told that I was not getting the job of computer room supervisor because I was too young and female, and instead, I would be working for someone I did not respect and whose ass I would have to save every day. I quit.

I started to work for another small computer company, which

operated in binary, and learned to read binary on a screen bending over my (by then) pregnant tummy.

Baby Leslie was born late in 1963, husband Dale was finishing his MSc, and I got a job working from home, writing the newspaper advertising for Hudson's Bay Company. I had my typewriter and Leslie in a plastic tilting chair beside me on the table. A taxi brought my work and took it back.

Dale was accepted at Stanford for PhD studies. We had a nine-month-old baby, and I got a job working at Stanford Research Institute as a computer applications analyst. I was living in a nervous state, wondering when I would have to tell my female boss I was pregnant again, at which point one of my worst parenting moments happened. I found out that the babysitter I had hired, and to whose home I took Leslie, was going out in the day and leaving Leslie alone, crying in her crib. That was it. If my baby could not be safe in California, I was going back to Canada. By then, all of the married students in Stanford housing knew what had happened, and an amazing woman came forward to take care of Leslie, and was her favorite person for the next three years. My boss didn't care that I was again pregnant and later that I'd had another baby. I would still come in at night and take the cover off the computer and manually fix the core if needed.

Next, I was back in Edmonton, with Dale teaching at the University of Alberta, and I being a housewife. I had another baby girl (now three kids in total) and stayed at home.

Housework was not my calling. However, to make up for the dirty dishes and unmade beds, I pursued a degree in education (which I did not finish because I could not complete the locum), set up the most disobedient Brownie Pack in history, became involved with the Committee for an Independent Canada (serving as local president), acted as a churchwarden, participated in Neighborhood Watch, and sewed and knitted.

I became seriously ill with asthma, and when I recovered, I had been replaced in all my jobs.

Since I had left computing, the field had completely passed me by.

Generations of computers had come and gone. So I went to law school. I had a nanny, and when the children were too old, I hired a woman who cooked up a storm and left me casseroles, cakes, and cookies. My teenaged daughters helped a lot and really pitched in when we adopted a four-year-old nephew.

I practiced law for 25 years and also taught. I was on some boards, wrote a couple of papers and articles, and enjoyed my work. I also spent hours on the edge of freezing soccer fields, cheering on our son.

While I was a lawyer, Dale was hired by Western University as a vice-president. All of the girls were in university or grown up, so our son and I traveled to London, Ontario. My credentials from Alberta were not accepted, so at fifty, I went back to school to take the bar exams for the Law Society of Upper Canada.

All this wisdom was observed and taken to heart by Penny's little sister, Sheelagh, yours truly.

CHAPTER FOUR

The Best Role Model Ever

I DIDN'T KNOW IT then, but Penny would have an outsized influence on me even by close-sister standards. I did take everything Penny said and did to heart. I still do.

Penny returned from her "gap" year working in England when I was nine. In the interim, our house had been set up with a stolid Yorkshire housekeeper, Mrs. Inch, who supplied me with a steady stream of *Girl's Own* weeklies and annuals that her relatives shipped from the UK, and ensured I developed a taste for workers' tea.

Around grade five, when I was eleven, my unique brand of whimsy no longer charmed my schoolmates, despite my ballet and art lessons and my selective willingness to "show them mine if they showed me theirs first." One day several of them rang the doorbell and when I came to the door, a longtime and once close playmate called Bill kicked me in the stomach. I am not sure if I was just shocked and winded or if I cried.

I don't remember mentioning the kick to anyone; life just went on.

In September of that year, I came home from school to find my mom, weakened by her MS, calling faintly to me from her bedroom upstairs. She informed me that the elementary school had called with news: they had decided I would be much happier skipping grade six and advancing, instead, to grade seven in the junior high school just down the road.

And advance I did, leaving childhood's realm for that of burgeoning adolescence. As it turned out, the sages' proclamation rang truer than the chimes of midnight—I was, indeed, much happier amid the hallowed company of my new, older peers in their school just down the road.

We all did our best. When a concerned junior high teacher asked why no one was signing up to attend my parent–teacher meetings, I replied, "We don't do that kind of thing in our family."

Amid the whirlwind of our ever-evolving household, my wise sister Penny, a university scholar now, assumed the mantle of ensuring we urchins were properly dressed and our tresses neatly plaited each morning. Not to be outdone, brother John, himself a seeker of knowledge, alongside his merry band of compatriots and Penny's own coterie of friends, embarked upon an ambitious endeavor—the construction of a shimmering oasis in our very backyard, its aquatic splendor engineered by the deft hand of our father, Dean. And once our pool shone forth in all its glory, a steady stream of local youths, some hailing from distant neighborhoods, would descend upon our humble porch, towels in hand, seeking refuge from the sun's scorching rays, their frolics overseen by a rotating cadre of lifeguards from the family—except for our matriarch, and youngest sister Terree, whose duties lay elsewhere.

Terree, my younger sister, had close friends—Bobby, Mary and Helen Frisch—who lived in the house across the street on the second floor. Some school days Terree and I were instructed to eat lunch at the Frisches and I still remember Mrs. Frisch's beans on toast and ice box cookies. Yummy.

Penny graduated and got married. John and I took turns feeding and watching over our mom evenings and weekends, Dean worked long hours at home and abroad to pay for the rising expenses of housekeepers and nurses. Terree became a bit eccentric while at the same time winning gold medals and trophies as a highland dancer and equestrian.

With John and Penny both gone, some evenings Terree and I tried to get our father to look up from reading *The Edmonton Journal* at the dinner table by having tongue races. (The person who said "go" had a serious disadvantage.) And we practiced curling our tongues. Terree could curl her tongue both lengthways and sideways *and* raise only one eyebrow while doing so. We had an early form of intercom in the kitchen so we could hear if Mom called. She had a sweet, soft voice and was sometimes hard to hear.

The highlight of those years was that, in addition to beans on toast, Mrs. Frisch provided another source of sustenance as the editor of *The Alberta Poetry Yearbook*. She encouraged me to submit poems, and my submission, "The Joy of Creation," made it into the yearbook one year. However, over the years, I have been most proud of "Oil!" which won an honorable mention and was featured on the last page of the 1964 edition of the yearbook.

As I learned much later, Leduc No. 1, a crude oil discovery just outside Edmonton, gushed in February 1947, two months before my birth. This discovery presaged the major development of oil in Alberta. The oil industry and its opportunities attracted Second World War refugees from Central Europe, who helped make Edmonton a vibrant city. Even at sixteen, when I wrote the poem, I must have felt the energy of this transformation.

Oil!

By Sheelagh Whittaker

They wiped their faces on dirt-stained rags
And the blazing sun beat on each metal hat.
All faces were tense as waiting, hoping,
They watched the drill and all prayed that
These six months of earnest working
Were for a reason—and there was a debt
That was owed to them by this hardened prairie,
But they watched the drill, and no sign came yet.

As they watched there, before their very eyes,
Came a black gold treasure, a reward for their toil,
And enemies shook hands and the hardest cried
For, from far and near came the cry of 'Oil!'

Perhaps this was a foretaste of my twenty-three years serving on the board of Imperial Oil.

CHAPTER FIVE

Aspiration Defined

THE DEDICATED EDUCATORS at Eastglen Composite High School ignited a spark in my subconscious, planting the seeds of ambition that would shape my future. In 1964, the television team quiz show *Reach for the Top* was very popular (and still is), especially among Edmonton high schoolers. It was an early version of quiz shows like *Mastermind*. Each school was represented by four grade 12 students with strong academic records. The choice of whom to select fell to the various high school administrators.

Typically schools were represented by four boys, three boys and a girl, or, in a pinch, two boys and two girls. In 1963, Eastglen was putting together its very first team, and it was decided that a general knowledge test would be given to all students who would like to represent the school. As it turned out, the successful competitors for a position on the team were all girls: Karen Zimmerman, Sharon Tucker, Lorraine Allison, and Sheelagh Whittaker. A four-girl team was virtually unheard of, and only two of us were on the official honor roll; even so, Eastglen stood by its process, and the four of us competed. The glass ceiling took notice.

We won some games and we lost some, and I embarrassed myself several times by being too eager to blurt out an answer that was incorrect. For example, in rapid response to a question that went something like "What do all these books have in common: *Lady Chatterley's Lover, 1984, Lord of the Flies, To Kill a Mockingbird* and . . .?" I pushed my buzzer and blurted out "They are all fiction," as quizmaster host Colin MacLean added, "*The Bible.*"

The shows were taped in advance, and I lived in agony of anticipation of the telecast where I would be revealed as a Christian non-believer—or just plain stupid. Luckily, when the tape was aired, the camera, at that moment, was focused on the quizmaster, not on our team, and a disembodied female voice gave the wrong answer. No one said anything, but I was very embarrassed.

The correct answer, I now know, is that the books on the list all had, at some time, been challenged or banned for standing in opposition to some people's social norms.

On my kitchen wall hangs a photo from one of the telecasts, featuring two teams displayed above their respective school names, the quizmaster, and our final scores (we won that one). This photo continues to serve as an exhortation for me to challenge myself and defy social conventions.

Reach For The Top

CHAPTER SIX

The Theatre of the Absurd as a Touchstone

I WAS JUST SEVENTEEN when I went to the University of Alberta to study English and history, living at home with my sister Terree, my father, Dean, who was often away, and Mom. The household also included our current housekeeper, Mrs. Yates of Lancashire, and Mary the Irish nurse, and the weekly cleaner we called Beatie (possibly short for Beatrice, though I never knew for sure). Beatie's husband beat her (definitely no pun intended), and then showed up during her workday to get the money that she had thus far earned. Meanwhile, I dated the man who would become my husband.

Despite my best efforts, I found studying second-year university French quite challenging. I did, however, enjoy my exposure to the Theatre of the Absurd in the form of Samuel Beckett's play *En attendant Godot* (*Waiting for Godot* in English). Enigmatic Lucky, who was enslaved to Pozzo, enthralled me with his paradoxical nature. Bound by a rope and subject to Pozzo's cruel whip, Lucky oscillates between profound silence and a sudden, mesmerizing torrent of words.

Certainly, back then I didn't really understand *Waiting for Godot*, and I am not sure I do now. I identified with Lucky, because he tries to be entertaining and yet he is caught up in an existential world that often makes no sense. Perhaps coincidentally, I, too, had experiences in which I was caught up in what I imagined as an absurdist scene from a Godot-like home life and thrust into a working environment often filled with characters like Vladimir and Estragon.

Around that time, elegant to the end, Mom slipped away.

We had lived so long in the steady state of my mother's invalidism that it seemed strange that it had ended. Now, more than sixty years later I can attest that the grieving, like the illness, is attenuated. I miss her now as much as ever.

Not long after her death, my choice of geography as a second-year option revealed itself to be a big mistake, and I dropped out of the study of climate and land masses and enrolled in extra courses and summer courses to graduate instead with a BSc in textiles chemistry. To this day I have only a very vague notion of where I am on the globe, or if I am hot.

I think textiles chemistry was a gesture toward employability. I had long enjoyed fashion and design and making my own clothes and knitting and chemistry, a strange combination but my own.

As graduation loomed, the student newspaper dropped a linguistic bombshell: our university motto, *Quaecumque vera*, supposedly meant, "If you want to, man, you can." Lacking any Latin prowess and brimming with naive trust, I swallowed this "translation" hook, line, and sinker. It wasn't until years later that I discovered the true meaning: "Whatsoever things are true." A motivational downgrade this. The actual translation, while perhaps more dignified, packed less of an inspirational punch.

The student newspapers' version seemed like a good motto to me, and still does. And I understood "man" to be generic.

Emboldened by this misinterpreted motto and its spirit of boundless possibility, I embraced life's adventures with youthful enthusiasm.

After graduating at the tender age of twenty, I jumped into matrimony with someone I believed was "the love of my life." Unfortunately, it didn't unfold as I had envisioned. Our whirlwind romance included a grand European adventure, where I found myself bewildered by an intimidating Orangemen's Walk in Londonderry and caught in the midst of a student and workers' strike in Paris that had effectively paralyzed the country.

After we settled in Toronto, I began my MSc studies at the University of Toronto, while he pursued his articling as an accountant. Ten months later, we went our separate ways, both realizing that we had been poor judges of character.

CHAPTER SEVEN

Finally, Feminism Penetrates My Consciousness

WHILE MY FATHER had envisioned his daughters as well-educated wives and mothers, my sister Penny was balancing these expectations with a career. She worked as a programmer at the Stanford Research Institute in California, sending her daughter to daycare while her husband pursued his studies.

I, on the other hand, whimsically pursued an MSc at the University of Toronto and dropped out, despite being very interested in my master's project, an antibiotic finish for cellulosics, which are man-made fibers made from wood pulp. My thesis advisor and I were trying to create a revolutionary curative using hospital sheets. But my heart was not in the process. Instead, after looking about for new challenges, I transferred faculties and earned a BA in history and English, and then relocated to Guelph, Ontario, on the arm of a handsome nutrition professor from the southern United States whom I had met while he was teaching at UofT.

I made another attempt at earning an MSc, this time at the University of Guelph. My project involved developing a carbon monoxide detector for cars—a mesh impregnated with a chemical that would complete a circuit and activate a buzzer when exposed to high levels of CO. Initially, I thought it was a fascinating project. However, as I conducted my research using outdated equipment, including an antiquated fume hood and an ill-fitting gas mask, I began to realize the inherent risks. The dangerous nature of working with carbon monoxide, combined with inadequate safety measures, led me to reconsider my path. Recognizing that I lacked the reckless determination of a Sylvia Plath, I decided to discontinue my studies once again.

In the meantime, however, I had read *The Alexandria Quartet* by Lawrence Durrell as well as Plath's *The Bell Jar* (of course) and pasted this Durrell quotation on the wall above my cubicle: "For those of us who stand upon the margins of the world, as yet unsolicited by any god, the only truth is that Work itself is Love."

And I found Work. I was hired to index the minutes of the University of Guelph's Senate and then, on a winning streak, those of the Board. My selection success was based chiefly on the readily demonstrated skill of saying the alphabet backward, and quickly.

It was during this period that I unknowingly chipped my first crack in the glass ceiling. I competed for and won the position of Assistant to the Provost at Guelph, a role previously held by a man. My triumph was short-lived. Almost immediately after my appointment, I received a call from HR that would forever etch certain numbers in my memory.

The HR representative explained that, as I was now a female "assistant to" in the position—same responsibilities, I presumed, only with a small "a" on "assistant"—my pay range would differ from what had been discussed during the selection process. The annual maximum for my position was now set at $7,500, a stark contrast to the $10,000 I had been promised.

Little did I know then that this experience would be just the first of many encounters with the invisible barriers women face in the workplace.

I had no bargaining chips, so I reluctantly accepted $7,500. Six months of hard work later, I approached my boss with a politely phrased demand: I would continue in my position if my salary were now raised to $10,500, which I had learned from reviewing the provost's files, now in my domain, was the amount that my predecessor had been paid. Otherwise, regretfully, I would have to resign.

And I meant it.

That was the first real test of my lifelong decision to never threaten anything I wouldn't actually do. It was going to be difficult, even heartbreaking, but it was a matter of principle.

My boss, the provost, tried to get me to empathize with his situation, reminding me, as I already knew, that he would have to make a special case to the president for such an unusual raise in the middle of the pay cycle. I acknowledged the difficulty of his situation but kept my resolve. A few days later, the provost stopped by my office to explain, sheepishly, that he had talked to the president and the highest he could go was $9,500 with a promise of $10,000 in the next cycle. Keeping in mind the wise advice of the philosopher and writer Balthasar Gracián, "Quit while you're ahead. All the best gamblers do," I smiled graciously, thanked the provost profusely, and accepted the deal. The overhead light, I recall, caught a flash of a tiny particle of glass dislodging from the ceiling.

While working my way up through to the role of Assistant to the Provost, I had joined my first Consciousness Raising Group, organized for faculty wives, librarians, senior administrative staff, and the occasional grad student. Meanwhile, I was blissfully oblivious to the fact that my desire to be taken seriously was undoubtedly being undermined by my wardrobe of brightly colored, polka-dot hot pants.

To prepare myself for what I expected to be challenging, even lively, discussions with the group, I read the feminist syllabus of the 1970s: Virginia Woolf, *A Room of One's Own*; Simone de Beauvoir, *The Second Sex*; Betty Friedan, *The Feminine Mystique*; Gloria Steinman, *Ms* magazine; German Greer, *The Female Eunuch*; Kate Millett, *Sexual Politics*; Robin Morgan, *Sisterhood Is Powerful*; and Erica Jong, *Fear of Flying*.

I had read *Madame Bovary* by Gustave Flaubert, in French, in an earlier life, but I am not sure I really got the point. And I couldn't get into *Our Bodies, Ourselves* by the Boston Women's Health Collective, but I had a copy.

My favorite was *Sisterhood Is Powerful*, by Robin Morgan. It was thoughtful and well written and avoided polemic.

And I could hum the anthem, "I am a Woman, hear me roar."

At the first meeting of our consciousness-raising group, held in the beautiful marital home of a male faculty member, we went around the room introducing ourselves. My vague recollection was that we were all very self-conscious and that our reasons for being there sounded pretty whiney. For example, "He won't help with the dishes," or, in my case, "He makes me water his hydroponic plants experiment while he vacations."

Our next meeting was not much better. However, the meetings began to get longer and more engaging, but they started to feel more and more like grievance sessions or gossip forums about faculty marriages. Finally, one insightful woman suggested that we start to focus on constructive ways to better our situations. As one witty would-be feminist, red-headed Bobbie, observed concerning our progress, "We have to learn to pull ourselves up by the hair on our legs."

Amazingly, through that autumn and winter, the University Lecture Series delivered first Betty Friedan, then Germaine Greer, and next Xaviera Hollander as speakers "in the flesh." The mainly female audience was mesmerized. Farley Mowat, whose books featured encounters with Arctic wolves, was the only male author on the agenda that I recall. Kind of an antidote, I guess.

The speakers in the series were memorable for their feminist credentials, but not particularly original in their arguments, except for a late entry, the television celebrity (later Canada's twenty-sixth governor-general) Adrienne Clarkson. Adrienne Clarkson advised her audience, in what felt like an edict: "In the language of the Quakers, be a witness to the life to which you believe you are entitled."

That instruction certainly resonated with me. I determined to be a witness.

As the Women's Liberation movement revved up, the university administration took its first tentative steps toward addressing gender equality. It established a small, but pivotal, Equal Opportunities Committee, consisting of just four members. I was fortunate to be appointed as the representative for non-academic staff, giving me a front-row seat to these groundbreaking discussions.

One particularly fascinating addition to our group was Garney Henley, representing the athletics department. Henley, a Canadian Football League legend and holder of the Most Outstanding Player award, brought a unique perspective to our meetings. His presence underscored the university's attempt to bridge diverse sectors in addressing gender equality. However, Henley's packed game schedule often made it challenging for him to attend our sessions, highlighting the ongoing struggle to prioritize these crucial conversations amid competing demands.

Our small committee, with its eclectic mix of members, embodied both the promise and the challenges of the university's nascent efforts to grapple with the complexities of gender equality in academia.

Progress was painfully slow. By the time I moved on from the university, the Equal Opportunities Committee had achieved only one significant milestone: getting its terms of reference approved.

CHAPTER EIGHT

Things I Did in Business School (not all of them, of course)

IT GOES WITHOUT saying that universities are hotbeds of good-looking, intelligent young people, and so looking back it is no surprise that an attractive student body leader convinced my hot-panted body to leave Guelph and accompany him in studying for an MBA. In the spirit of the song "Anything you can do, I can do better" from the previously referenced *Annie Get Your Gun* musical, I decided to get an MBA, too.

The fact that Germaine Greer, Gloria Steinman, Erica Jong, *et al.* would likely approve was reassuring. As for Betty Friedan, I'm not so certain. At this point Betty was starting to be a bit "old school."

Mike (the student body leader who accompanied me from Guelph) and I were fortunate to secure scholarships, supplemented by our modest savings. We set our sights on the newly constructed York University Business School—not yet known as the Schulich School, and still missing an elevator. For a young woman like me, the timing couldn't have been more opportune to pursue an MBA.

By my estimation, my female classmates and I were among the first fifty women in Canada to earn this degree. In my graduating class alone, there were eight or nine of us—a small, but significant, cohort. Our novelty in this male-dominated field worked to our advantage: both faculty and fellow students treated us with a surprising degree of fairness and respect.

The incomplete state of the building, with its missing elevator, seemed to mirror the evolving landscape of business education—still under construction, but rapidly advancing. As we navigated the halls and classrooms, we were not just pursuing degrees, but unknowingly blazing trails for future generations of women in business.

On my first day, I hurried into the washroom before class, only to notice as I came out of the cubicle that there were urinals on the wall, some partially full. Horrified, I scurried out, not realizing I was simply "self-identifying" years ahead of my time.

Mike, the student body leader from Guelph, was an intelligent, charming, sensitive man who had the good sense to sit well away from me in any classes we shared, to the extent that it was halfway through first year before some of our classmates realized that we were living together. He was the epitome of the new man; while competitive, he was not competitive with me, and he genuinely seemed not to care between us who got higher marks (I cared). I also made friends with a smart guy called Bram, who sat with me late into the night and talked about life while we waited for our turn to use the single computer available to us all and taught me how to pronounce "bagel." He was promised to a woman whom we never saw in two years of study, but I checked on him recently, and they did, in fact, get married.

Many of our courses were general management and strategy courses, and I focused on managerial finance, economics, and marketing, all of which were comparatively new to me, while Mike was particularly interested in operations research.

Most major assignments at York rightly emphasized teamwork, which was definitely the best way to educate us for the workplace but led to some rather humorous outcomes. For example, one young man in our working group earned his share of our mark by getting his girlfriend to type up our final submission. Rather than being bothered by that, we were grateful she was willing to do it.

And we were young and feisty, so we gave our teams provocative names like "Moose Pasture" and "Bullshit Enterprises." The latter had a biggish team of six high-scoring GMAT (the business school aptitude test) members and we took on a large imaginary task to help a company market a new product. The goal was to improve the company's balance sheet. Well, somehow, we did almost everything wrong and finally resorted to human capital accounting—a method that quantifies the economic value of employees' skills and knowledge—to beef up our numbers.

We got a C on the project, but our accounting prof had the grace to tell us we would have received a C- if we had not worked in the human capital accounting.

In the autumn of first year, I read a notice on the bulletin board about a York-Laval Business School Exchange Program. It was an opportunity to go to Quebec at the end of first year, take French courses, and work for a Quebec employer, while completing the third semester of your MBA program in French, and then return to York for your last semester. And it offered a $1,500 subsidy to qualified applicants. It sounded wonderful to a woman who had been taught French in Alberta and was running low on funds.

Excited, I went home and described the program to Mike, and he immediately said, "Yes." (We were like that: decisive.) And the following April, there we were, on the Plains of Abraham.

Mike and I had a wonderful little apartment on Rue St. Ursule. Two French professors from Lebanon, where the quality of spoken French was considered to be superior to that in Quebec, were hired by Laval to spend an intensive first month with the students from York—teaching language and grammar, ordering and eating in restaurants, and having fun. Then we spent the time until classes started working; my job in the Quebec government was interesting and challenging. Our social circle included one female York colleague, five male York colleagues, and one of their wives.

As it turned out, there were two saving graces for those of us who were in the exchange program. While lectures were in French, the textbooks for business education in North America are generally written in English. At Laval, exam questions are normally written in French; however, if you are lucky enough to understand the question, you are allowed to respond to it in English.

We returned from Quebec with one wife, one Quebec girlfriend, one female York student, four male York students (one decided to go skiing), plus Mike and me with a baby *in utero*. (I have always said she has *fabriqué au Québec* on the sole of her foot.)

Back in Toronto, I faced one of the first tests of my feminist principles when we had to tell Mike's parents about the impending baby. I really loved Mike's mother, Kay, a traditional practicing Roman Catholic of Irish extraction, and I didn't want to disappoint her with an illegitimate first grandchild, but there we were. She was amazing. She took my hand and said, "Well, Sheelagh, it isn't what I'd want for my daughter, but as long as you two are happy, I'm happy." (The fact that Mike was still married to someone else probably also played a role.)

The rest of Mike's family took their cue from her.

On my side of the family, at that time our father Dean's grandchildren to date were Penny's three daughters, all with their father's last name. Penny advised me to point out to our father that he now had a chance to have a grandchild—maybe even a grandson—with his last name. He seemed happy with that. (I didn't say anything about hyphenated naming options.) We all forgot about John's two boys and a girl being Whittakers—they were far away in Nova Scotia where John was teaching engineering. Out of sight, out of mind.

Taking classes to complete my last semester, I had a new, more accommodating wardrobe but enjoyed no special treatment. It was hard work but a lot of fun. I took a course called Entrepreneurial Undertakings and chose for this course to develop the detailed start-up plans for a folksy bookstore in a small town like Elmira, Ontario (with a population under 10,000). The plan was to have the bookstore on the main floor of a big old house and the baby nearby in the living quarters upstairs. It *was* educational to interview book suppliers, bookstore operators, and clerks, but in the final analysis I calculated that, with my education, I would have an easier time and make more money working as a banker or a salesperson or a government employee.

Speaking of which, Career Planning and Placement invited an array of potential employers to campus, and I interviewed with several. I was quite interested in a banking position but the bank in question decided that they were not that interested in me. I applied for a job in Combines Investigation for the federal government; I wasn't that sure what the job entailed but it sounded interesting. They were looking to hire law graduates, MBAs, and economists to make up highly skilled teams of anti-trust investigators to tackle their increasingly complex cases ranging from business price fixing to bid-rigging.

The interview was in Ottawa, and I carefully chose my most businesslike maternity dress (almost an oxymoron) and flew off to be interviewed. The interviewers were encouraging and made the job sound very interesting, and I returned home that evening full of hope. The man beside me on the plane, in whom I confided my excitement that the prospect seemed real, regardless of my condition, grumpily said that they probably just didn't have the wit to notice that I was pregnant. I wrote him off as unenlightened.

Whatever the case, I got the job and permission to start in September when the baby would be three months old. In those days, the feds were looking for ostensibly bilingual personnel and for senior females, so it appeared that the winds of gender equality and language égalité were blowing in my favor.

Not long after, Mike got a job with *The Financial Post* in Montreal, which posed a new challenge since my job was in Ottawa. But we were optimistic that we could find a solution to the living place problem.

Final exams were a bit tricky since my girth kept me well back from the edge of the desk. In those days we didn't use computers and some exams were written in longhand. And we shared an early version of small calculating machines. My last exam was Managerial Finance and the increasingly restless baby within managed to position itself so that with one sharp kick it sent my exam booklet flying off the desk. The invigilator picked up the exam and brought it to me anxiously, whispering, "Are you alright?"

"Yes. I just have three more questions to go," I whispered urgently, before setting back to work. As I recall, Embryo and I got quite a good mark.

We all graduated—Mike, baby girl, and I, although the doctor wouldn't let me take a twelve-day-old baby to the official ceremony. The hat would have been too big for her anyway.

One last incident of note. When my new baby girl Meghan was about three weeks old, I got an interesting phone call from one of my fellow graduates, a pleasant, bright, hardworking married man who had stayed back at York studying while some of us were off learning French. I still had my nightie on, although it was almost noon, and my front was wet from milk, but fortunately this was well before phones with video.

I wondered why he was calling; he had never called me before, but I assumed he wanted to speak to Mike, who was not home. "No," he said, "I want to talk to you. I was wondering now that the course is finished if you might consider being my mistress."

"Dumbfounded" would be a good word to describe my reaction. I had been raised to be polite, so I believe I said, "Well thank you for asking, but as you know I have just had a baby, and Mike and I will likely be moving to Ottawa." He bid me a disappointed goodbye.

Mike shrugged when I told him about the call and said, "At least he has good taste."

CHAPTER NINE

Things I Learned in Business School

DURING MY STUDIES, I encountered Burton Malkiel's Random Walk Theory, which initially seemed confined to the realm of stock market forecasting. Malkiel posits that stock prices move in an unpredictable manner, rendering past trends useless for future predictions. As I delved deeper, I realized this concept had a far broader application, one that resonated profoundly with my own life experiences.

My education, career trajectory, and even my romantic endeavors seemed to embody this theory of unpredictability. Like the erratic movements of stock prices, the short-term fluctuations in my life often defied any attempt at forecasting. Each decision, each relationship, each career move appeared to be influenced by a complex interplay of random events and unforeseen circumstances.

Just as Malkiel's theory challenges the notion that historical stock data can reliably predict future market behavior, my life's journey has repeatedly demonstrated that short-term patterns or experiences aren't necessarily indicative of long-term outcomes. This realization was both liberating and humbling, reminding me that life, much like the stock market, is full of surprises and unexpected turns.

In embracing this "personal random walk," I've come to appreciate the futility of trying to rigidly plan every aspect of my future based on past events. Instead, I've learned to remain adaptable, open to new opportunities, and resilient in the face of unpredictable changes—skills that serve well in both personal life and the ever-fluctuating world of business and finance.

I learned how to do a lot of work in a short period of time.

I learned that men can be completely comfortable with a pregnant woman in their midst, and can even find her attractive, as long as she doesn't take up too much space.

I learned that babies, at least singly, are portable.

I learned that if you want to make a lot of money, starting and running a small business is a hard way to accomplish it.

I learned that none of us is as smart as all of us in a team—but you can still go wrong, even if you use human capital accounting.

I learned that my received version of the University of Alberta motto—"If you want to, man, you can"—was still operative for me.

CHAPTER TEN

The Singular of Premises Is Not "Premise"

SOMEWHERE IN MY youth or childhood, some of my Spidey senses must have suffered mutation, because while I can be very sensitive to my environment, I can also be downright oblivious. Happily for me, that insensitivity has spared me much angst.

One of the things I didn't understand when I took the job with the federal Competition Bureau as a Combines Investigation Officer was that there was a lot of travel required in that position. Similarly, I had barely grasped that as investigators, we were responsible for vetting complaints, developing theories of cases, conducting preliminary investigations, performing on-site searches, writing case summaries, working with prosecution teams to further develop cases, attending trials, occasionally serving as witnesses, and suggesting penalties to Ministry of Justice lawyers for business crimes ranging from bid-rigging to price maintenance. We also had a role in enforcing the Foreign Investment Review Act. The position was a crash course in the intricacies of business law and investigative practices, demanding a level of versatility and expertise I hadn't initially anticipated.

Not only did you need to manage your own cases and prosecution follow-up, you were also responsible for helping other officers do their simultaneous searches when the search order specified premises in several cities or provinces. Not ideal for a young mother with a three-month-old baby. Nevertheless, it turned out I loved the job. As sister Penny remarked to others, "Of course she loves the job, she always was snoopy."

Mike and I made an offer on a house in Ottawa after discovering that suitable accommodation for a family with a baby was difficult to find near the bus station so that he could commute to Montreal. We crammed ourselves (Mike, me, the baby, and a mosquito) into a call box in Ottawa and called Mike's parents to ask if they would lend us $10,000 for a down payment on the house. Then we rented a studio apartment on Mountain Street in Montreal so Mike could stay over on his newspaper deadline nights.

I hired a nanny to look after baby Meghan while I was at work in Ottawa, but soon after I found I had to conduct the search for my first case at a premises in Montreal. A "premises" in the singular was investigation jargon to refer to a physical location or property where a business operates or where evidence related to an investigation may be found. This Montreal travel was agreeable because Mike had to be on assignment elsewhere, so I had use of the apartment with the baby, and his secretary's sister agreed to babysit if I could get the baby to her in a northern Montreal suburb before 8 in the morning.

Early on search day, already ensconced in Montreal, the Combines team of four officers, all in our late twenties, set off in a rented car to go to the premises in question, via Mike's secretary's sister's house to drop off the baby. Then we proceeded to the search sites. I was accompanied by a charming young man from Brandon, Manitoba, on this, my first, search. We were dropped off and the others journeyed to the second site with plans to pick us up later.

As we arrived with a search order in hand, we saw a woman on a stretcher being removed from the premises. We were told later that her husband had beaten her the night before and she had collapsed at work.

Once ushered into the president's office, I proffered my warrant and told him politely that we were about to go through his files, logs, briefcase, desk, daybook, and other relevant materials, and those of his staff.

He picked up the phone and called his lawyer:

"I have in my office a well-dressed young man, probably college-educated, and an attractive woman with a search warrant. What should I do?"

After some formalities, we were allowed to proceed. (Some beginnings you never forget.)

That evening, after we had all gone to pick up Meghan, we reconvened at the Coffee Mill Hungarian Restaurant for dinner. Meghan, who had not yet been weaned, sat in her baby car seat on a chair at the table, waiting patiently. We had a lot of laughs, especially after the well-dressed young man, educated at the University of Manitoba, had his chance to tell the story of our serving of the search order. Then we went off to our lodgings, agreeing to finish the job the next morning. To the best of my recollection, of the three male officers working with me, no one commented on the baby joining us for dinner.

That case was my first successful prosecution.

I really enjoyed the job of Combines Investigation Officer. It was varied and could be stressful and I realized early on that interesting work experiences in Combines occurred in inverse proportion to your rank. The more senior you became, the more time you had to spend in dreary administration.

I started off as a Commerce Officer One, Development level (i.e., CO1D) pursuant to accepted nomenclature and the rules of our union, The Professional Institute of Public Servants (PIPS, for short). PIPS was my only experience as a union member, and it was very enlightening. I never before had worked in a world with such explicit constraints and entitlements. My salary was $16,300 per year.

The general expectation was that most CO1s would graduate quickly out of the D category and on to greater things, CO4 being the highest designation before one reached the senior managerial ranks and thereby became a serious part of the administrative hierarchy.

A competition for CO3s had been held shortly before I arrived and a precious few had been appointed. By my recollection they were all rather tall young men. Truth be told, no one expected me or my female friends, Sandra and Suzanne, ever to make it to CO3.

The administration liked Sandra best because she was smart and unobtrusive and from Vancouver. They liked Suzanne second best because she was perfectly bilingual and had *joie de vivre*.

We worked comparatively hard, and, at one point, my conviction record was seven out of six: the judge had inadvertently convicted a company listed as an unindicted co-conspirator on the charge. It took some finesse on the part of the lawyer for the Crown to clear that up.

Things were not working perfectly smoothly. One senior director (a CO4) was not totally comfortable with me in the job, and when my own chief (also a CO4) rated me as "excellent" in my annual performance review, that senior director had the review document sent back, complaining that there was insufficient supporting information in the document to justify the rating of "excellent." (He must have stayed up late working on that justification for downgrading me.) So, I was downgraded to "fully satisfactory." As is sometimes the case, I was in possession of all of the details of this to-and-froing because a likable CO3 of my acquaintance kept me up to date during the entire spurious process.

I cried on the way home from work.

After some more time and struggle I made it to the rank of CO2.

I did, I confess, commit some serious workplace errors. I didn't understand the sanctity of "chain of command" and I was flattered when a senior lawyer reached around my direct boss to ask me about a case. Big mistake, especially if your boss was a veteran of the Second World War. He bridled at a member of his team talking to "Justice" (a.k.a. the Minister's ambit) without his involvement.

However, getting a half day off to go Christmas shopping for a present for the boss to give to his wife felt like a real perk, and I am sure she was grateful for the beautiful satin blouse I chose. My peers raised their eyebrows.

As workplace struggles and minor intrigues began to weigh on both of us, Mike and I decided to plan for another baby. We hoped this would provide a welcome diversion for Meghan and ourselves.

By this time, my colleagues and I had grown quite comfortable with each other—an inevitable result of a group of nearly thirty-year-olds working in close proximity due to our cost-saving open office design. This casual atmosphere sometimes led to unexpected moments of amusement.

One day, my boss received a critique from a senior outside counsel regarding some case discussion points I had prepared in anticipation of a meeting with him. Rather than discussing the strength of "Mr. Whittaker's arguments" privately, he chose to read the lawyer's commentary aloud from his desk, sharing it with everyone in the office. His hearty laughter echoed through our workspace as he relayed the counsel's pointed observations about my work.

"I can't wait until he gets to meet '*Mr.* Whittaker,'" he chortled.

I still remember what I had on that day, a navy and white fine-checked maternity jumper and blouse that I imagined looked quite businesslike but was, in fact, rather form-fitting now that I was eight months pregnant.

This incident, while potentially embarrassing, exemplified the informal and sometimes unconventional dynamics of our office environment. It also highlighted the challenges of maintaining professional boundaries in such an open setting, where private feedback could easily become public knowledge.

It was my plan to work right up to the birth, which was due, rather serendipitously, around ten days after daughter Meghan's second birthday. So it was somewhat to my surprise when I went into labor on her birthday, and one of my colleagues had to drive me to the Grace Hospital. It was a Friday. But the baby changed its mind, held out for a birthday of his own, and by evening, Mike drove me home.

Saturday, Sunday, and Monday passed in a haze of boredom. Tuesday morning, my boss phoned to see what I was doing.

"Nothing," I sighed.

"Well then get the hell in here, we need you," he said. (He talked like that.)

So, in I went, and son Matthew was born the following Sunday, right on schedule.

While I was in the hospital, two interesting things happened. My boss arrived, with fanfare, at my bedside with a beautifully wrapped, charming green corduroy jumpsuit for the new baby. Later that day, a pleasant, well-dressed woman came to my bedside and made friends with me. I thought maybe she was a volunteer hospital visitor. Then she surprised me by saying, sweetly, "Well, I am sure we are not going to let this happen again, are we, dear?"

I looked at her blankly. "Let what happen?" I asked.

"Have another baby without a daddy, of course," she replied. "Our records show that this is your second child and that you are unmarried. You don't want to go through life like that, do you?"

It turns out that she had been assigned by the hospital as my social worker to help me align with the societal values of the day (this being in the year 1977). I really liked her and promised to try to do better in future. And I never had a child out of wedlock again, if you don't count adoption.

Mike had moved from reporter to special assistant to a cabinet minister, so our household was now anchored in Ottawa. We had a new nanny, and I stayed home and mothered for a bit. But I was working on a particularly interesting case, and so, while I had saved up my vacation leave to stay at home for six weeks, I went back to work after about a month. Finances were tight. The concept of doing serious work from home had not yet been normalized.

Like many of my colleagues, I was an assiduous reader of the PIPS's *Union Handbook*, and, at that time, it included an interesting benefit in the "Special Leave for Members" section. It stipulated that a special leave circumstance allowed for one day of extra leave if there was a family situation that could not be dealt with "by anyone else in any other way at any other time." *Aha*, I thought, I will claim a day of paid leave for the birth of my son.

I applied for a day of special leave through HR and eventually learned that my application had been denied. After some consideration, I involved the union, a rather cumbersome process. More time passed. I was duly informed that they declined to support me, despite the fact that one example of special leave offered in the PIPS handbook was being needed to drive a wife home from the hospital after childbirth.

Somewhere along the line I heard reports of concerned conversations about how permission for such leave might cause an outbreak of pregnancy among female employees. Even as I type this, I can't imagine anyone would seriously consider this a possibility, but it seemed as if many people actually did at the time.

At this point, my boss, the former military man, took me aside and said: "Sheelagh, keep on grieving up the chain. I will approve it and when it finally gets to the Deputy Minister (at that time, a groundbreaking female appointee) she will approve that day of leave."

I refiled my grievance and heard nothing—ever. However, when I received my annual notification of vacation days outstanding, it looked like there was one more day than I would otherwise have expected.

The next couple of years at the Bureau of Competition Policy were interesting and exciting. Mike, the kids, and I moved house again. I was the officer in charge of a couple of landmark cases, and I got to work with giants of the legal profession like J.J. Robinette. It was fascinating and challenging work, and I was learning new things every day.

One day at lunch midway through a lengthy predatory-pricing case, Edward Sexton, the distinguished counsel leading the government's case, turned to me in a rare moment of frustration and said, "Sheelagh, there is not a rule for everything. Sometimes things just are."

I was not particularly abashed. I like to learn new things.

A few years after I left Combines, I invited my former boss to lunch at The Green Valley Restaurant when I was on a job in Ottawa. It was a lovely lunch, complete with old-fashioned goodies like boiled cabbage and candid reminiscing. When we were winding up, he said, "You know, Sheelagh, we were not always as fair to you as we should have been. I am sorry for that."

Bemused, I bid him a fond goodbye.

CHAPTER ELEVEN

A Feminist Family Anthem

RECENTLY, A LONGTIME friend of mine, an exceptionally successful woman, asked me to define feminism. As I glanced around her inviting living space, where her husband was preparing a delicious lunch for us, I thoughtfully replied, "Free to be you and me."

Both members of the couple looked at me with quizzical expressions.

"Yes," I continued, "the *Marlo Thomas and Friends* album had it right. I especially liked the song *Parents Are People*.

Parents Are People

Mommies are people,
People with children.
When mommies were little, they used to be girls,
Like some of you, but then they grew . . .

And the mirror verse.

Daddies are people,
People with children.
When daddies were little, they used to be boys
Like some of you, but then they grew . . .

"The voice needs work, but the sentiment sounds good," said my girlfriend.

"Free to Be . . . You and Me" was released in 1972, the same year *Ms.* magazine launched and just a year before I began business school. As toddlers, my children, Meghan and Matthew, loved singing along to songs. However, Matthew had a particular fondness for a Smurf song that went, "Beer, beer, smurfing beer, you don't get drunk and it isn't dear." Until now, I had mistakenly thought the lyric was, "you don't get drunk and you disappear."

The Smurf songs were on a long-playing record, and one day it just slipped from my hand and fell to the floor, breaking. I swear that was a true accident; even my subconscious denies liability for it.

That phrase, "Free to be . . . you and me," still seems to epitomize what feminism is all about—for both men and women.

CHAPTER TWELVE

Keep Trying until You Get It Right

A NEW AND EXCITING opportunity for Mike at a Toronto-based company decided our next move. My own attitude was that, much as I enjoyed Combines Investigation, and I did, the business credibility from my MBA was going to expire pretty soon if I didn't gain some experience in the actual world of business.

My good friend Lawson Hunter, a Justice lawyer who later became a renowned figure in Canadian competition law, suggested I explore opportunities with a management consulting firm in Toronto. He believed the firm was brimming with brilliant minds and thought I might fit in well as a consultant. Lawson took the initiative to recommend me to them as well.

The interviews that followed were truly captivating. The Canada Consulting Group (CCG) had been founded by a group of astute McKinsey alumni and other accomplished young business professionals. Their vision was to offer consulting services within Canada, with a particular focus on government work—an area that McKinsey, at the time, showed little interest in pursuing, at least not in Canada.

This introduction opened a door to a world where business acumen met public sector challenges, presenting an intriguing opportunity for my career trajectory.

After four or five meetings over coffee or lunch, they had me hooked on consulting. Luckily for me, they did most of the talking. Once hooked,

I discreetly asked around to find out who McKinsey was and why they were so admired.

Years later, I learned that Lawson had given me the following reference: "She's bright but undisciplined."

In retrospect, that reference seems fair to me. I'm a bit more disciplined now, but not a lot.

My first day at Canada Consulting began with my falling down my front porch steps and denting my beautiful new burgundy leather briefcase. I was welcomed into more open offices and began to do whatever I was assigned. I had no particular reputation, and the only business I brought in was a contract to finish the litigation of my bid-rigging case at Combines.

Canada Consulting had already had a female consultant, and they were happy for me to be simply Ms. Whittaker. The fact that I was an unmarried mother of two never came up; it was almost 1980, and Canada was pretty progressive in those days. I had no burning urge to shine; I just wanted to fit in. I was very impressed with how smart and hardworking everyone was, and I simply focused on measuring up to the standard.

David Maister, in his excellent book *Managing the Professional Service Firm*, describes three types of consulting: Brains, Grey Hair, and Procedure.

Brains firms offer new, innovative ideas. Grey Hair firms offer the benefit of experience. Procedure firms offer standardized execution.

Canada Consulting Group was a "Brains" firm. Working there as a junior consultant was paradise to me. No one expected me to really know what I was doing; all I was supposed to do was learn, learn, learn; think, think, think; and work, work, work.

Evenings in our Cabbagetown-area house in Toronto typically went like this: We ate prosaic family meals, prepared at our request by the nanny. Then we'd watch "The Dukes of Hazzard," "Family Ties," or "Transformers," which had a character named Megatron who disdainfully referred to a co-worker as a "dipstick tape deck." After kissing the kids goodnight, I'd pull out my work papers on the sofa and use my stomach as a desk. (This was long before the common use of computers and shortly after people in my family had ceased to refer to a random writing surface, such as one's stomach, as a "hard.")

I felt well remunerated, and I liked working with clients. I lacked the aplomb of later recruit, the late business and civic leader, David Pecaut, who joined CCG straight out of Harvard, and who, when asked at his very first client meeting how long he had been with the firm, replied, "I'm still completing my first year."

Little wonder he has a park in downtown Toronto named after him.

I was teased for having "generic brand" credentials, but with the help of the partners and my own curiosity, I made steady progress. Occasionally, I would point out to a snooty CCG Ivy Leaguer that Yale had only voted to accept female students in November 1969, two years *after* I had earned my BSc.

One day, a senior CCG colleague and I were standing by the exit door talking, when one of the more junior consultants passed by on his way out. He stopped briefly when I asked him how his wife's internship was going, if his client had liked his new cost-saving idea, and if he was playing hockey on Friday. My colleague stared, first at me, then at our younger colleague, and said to him, "How does she know all this stuff about you?"

The junior, who also had Ivy League credentials, stopped and said simply, "She asks."

I was very fortunate in my initial assignments and in the consultants I worked with. As I began to get the hang of things, I was asked to partner with Neil, one of our brilliant founders, to consult for a special committee of Parliament. This committee had been created to answer a crucial question: Should Canada establish a national trading corporation, possibly modeled after the famous Japanese trading companies like Mitsubishi? What a memorable experience and learning adventure that turned out to be!

Our committee was composed of three male and one female Liberal MPs (including the chair), two Conservatives, and one member of the NDP. Our task was formidable.

The question we had to answer was a good one. With Canada's trade relationships severely skewed toward the United States, it was timely to investigate how we might reduce our trade dependency on a single partner.

Neil and I, with input from the committee, worked out a grueling schedule of hearings and interviews to learn what kind of new, mutual trade relationships might be developed for Canada. A major working hypothesis was that Canada's strength in executing engineering capital projects abroad could serve as a suitable base for expanded foreign trade. At that time, engineering companies like Siemens, Sandvik, SNC, Lavalin, China Engineers, and Kone were the titans of global capital project companies, two of which, SNC and Lavalin, were Canadian.

It was agreed that the committee would hold public and private hearings in the US, across Canada, and at locations in Europe. We started in New York, where the vice president of a major investment company told us privately, over at the side table laid out with coffee and croissants, that Canada would never succeed in significantly improving its trade balance because Canadians don't know how to "kick ass."

Our international mission then began in earnest. Neil and I often divided the delegates to cover more ground, each leading a small entourage to countries selected by committee members. After Paris, our paths diverged. I embarked on a journey to Prague, Belgrade, and Hamburg, accompanied by a diverse trio: a Conservative, a Liberal, and an NDP member.

Some of our experiences were, to put it mildly, eye-opening. In Paris, at the recommendation of the Embassy, we found ourselves at the Crazy Horse, known for its provocative topless performances. Later, in Hamburg, we explored the infamous Reeperbahn, a district notorious for its adult entertainment, illicit substances, and sex work.

These visits with backbench MPs to such colorful establishments were certainly memorable, if not entirely aligned with our official duties.

After our return, we completed our hearings across Canada. One evening, long after midnight, I found myself in St. John's checking into a hotel across town from the hearings site. The hotel we had reserved at the site had only two rooms left, and neither the NDP member, the Liberal member, nor I would agree to share. Nor could we split up. After our hearings in Quebec, they had jointly given me a book entitled *Have a Taste of Sheila*, which the store sold pre-wrapped in cellophane. I pointed out that if it were for me, my name was spelled incorrectly. (It is not acceptable for any of us to do such things anymore.)

Back home, my colleague Neil and I sat down to structure what we all had learned and might reasonably conclude. With the approval of the committee, Neil assigned me to write chapter 5 of our final report. If I remember correctly, it was about recommendations concerning various trading initiatives, rules, and practices we had heard of or seen that might improve Canada's trading performance.

Obedient, if uninspired, I set about to write my chapter and submitted my draft. It was returned promptly with this single comment: "good start." So, I took up my pen anew (still pre-computer), thought up some new initiatives and recommendations, organized things a bit better, and sent it back to Neil.

Neil returned that draft with a "getting better," but he was too busy with his own chapters to discuss mine with me. Well, I am not a quitter, and I was determined to measure up.

So, I rewrote chapter 5 extensively and submitted it with a note that said, "I'm not sure what else I can add here." I got an "OK, now write chapter 2," in response. So, I did.

Subsequently, I learned that Henry Kissinger used a similar process once when dealing with his speech writer. Only his response to the third effort was "OK, now I'll read it."

Both Neil and I learned a lot from that chapter-by-chapter review, and we were comfortable thereafter whenever we undertook something new and difficult together.

Was that assignment a glass ceiling? Not quite. In fact, it was more of a launching pad. The entire experience helped me grasp what was considered the gold standard in our field, propelling me toward the upper echelons of consulting expertise. In the world of high-stakes consulting, when top-notch work is in demand, gender often takes a back seat to competence and results.

But the lessons weren't all about professional growth. I also gained some unexpected insights into the quirks and idiosyncrasies of various members of Parliament. One particular incident stands out: a parliamentarian who boarded our flight home sporting a wide streak of sparkles in his Brylcreem-slicked hair. It was a vivid reminder that even in the corridors of power, human nature can be delightfully unpredictable.

These experiences, both professional and personal, painted a complex picture of the world I was navigating. They underscored that success in business consulting wasn't just about expertise, but also about understanding the human element in all its glittering, sometimes absurd, glory.

CHAPTER THIRTEEN

A Swift One to the Ankle

SECURING THE CANTEL license for the partnership of Ted Rogers, Philippe de Gaspé Beaubien, and Marc Belzberg was a career-defining achievement. This experience taught me a valuable lesson: when you accomplish something remarkable, there's never a shortage of people eager to claim credit. Fortunately, in this instance, the key players were well aware of each individual's contributions.

The Cantel project marked a pivotal moment not only in Canadian telecommunications history but also in my professional journey. It underscored the value of perseverance, strategic thinking, and the ability to work effectively within a team of powerful personalities.

The race for Canada's first non-telco mobile service license was heating up, and the competition was fierce. Just two weeks before the application deadline, on an otherwise ordinary Friday, our phones rang with an unexpected opportunity. Ted, Philippe, and Marc were on the line, their voices brimming with determination. They had a bold request: they wanted to hire us to secure the coveted license for them.

As soon as the call ended, Jerome, my CCG partner, reminded me of his upcoming skiing trip with his son. The clock was ticking, and we knew we had to act fast. With a mix of excitement and urgency, we dove headfirst into planning mode. For the rest of that day, we worked feverishly, outlining the monumental task that lay ahead. Our minds raced with strategies and possibilities as we sketched out a road map to victory.

With our initial blueprint in place, Jerome set off for his father–son adventure, leaving me to carry the torch. The challenge ahead was daunting, but the thrill of potentially shaping the future of Canadian mobile services fueled our determination. As I watched Jerome leave, I couldn't help but feel a surge of anticipation for the intense weeks that lay ahead.

For a while, I genuinely believed that I had sacrificed years of my life for that project. The intensity of the drama was palpable. We secured special premises and burned the midnight oil. On the final Saturday, Jerome and I found ourselves in a suburban copy shop that had graciously agreed to stay open just for us, alongside David Lint, the investors' representative. We spent the entire night photocopying applications in both English and French, meticulously tailored for five different regions. As the clock struck five, we finally completed our monumental task, exhausted but exhilarated by the effort we had poured into this venture.

The final push to submit our applications was a whirlwind of activity. As evening fell, our team dispersed across the country for the crucial delivery phase. I found myself boarding a jet to Edmonton, my arms laden with hefty copies of the Alberta Applications for Cantel. This personal touch of hand-delivering to each region was intended to make a lasting impression on the Department of Communications.

Fatigue weighed heavily on me as I settled into my seat in the front row. Turning to the fellow beside me, I mustered what little energy I had left and said "I hope this won't bother you," before unceremoniously resting my head on his shoulder. Exhaustion took over, and I drifted off into a deep sleep that lasted the entire four-and-a-half-hour flight to Edmonton.

As we touched down, I awoke with a start, suddenly aware of my impromptu pillow. A wave of embarrassment washed over me as I realized the predicament I might have put my seatmate in. To this day, I can't help but wonder if he had needed to use the restroom during our journey, trapped by my slumbering form. The memory serves as a reminder of the lengths we went to and the unexpected kindness of strangers in our quest to secure the mobile service license.

Marc Belzberg was evidently impressed by Canada Consulting's performance, prompting him to explore the possibility of replicating our success with an investment venture in Israel. The project, cleverly dubbed "Isratel," unfortunately never progressed beyond the concept stage. During our work on the Isratel proposal, Marc shared an intriguing piece of information with me. He revealed that he had initially selected me to serve as his representative on the Cantel board. However, this plan was thwarted when he was informed that I lacked "sufficient experience" for the role.

The revelation of Marc's initial intention to appoint me to the Cantel board, juxtaposed with the subsequent rejection based on my perceived lack of experience, raised some interesting questions. It seemed puzzling given our recent success and the trust Marc had placed in our abilities.

The dismissal of his choice based on such grounds suggests that there may have been other factors at play in the decision-making process. Was this an innocuous reminder of the complex dynamics often at work in corporate governance and board appointments? Or of the sometimes-arbitrary nature of experience assessments, especially in rapidly evolving industries like telecommunications where innovative thinking and fresh perspectives can be as valuable as traditional experience? Or was it attributable to something inchoate, like the glass ceiling of that era?

Canada Consulting's client portfolio expanded over time, attracting a diverse and intriguing range of organizations. One of our most notable clients was the Canadian Broadcasting Corporation (CBC), a prestigious account whose assignments I particularly enjoyed. The CBC, as Canada's national broadcaster, held iconic status among the boomer generation and entrusted us with several of its ambitious projects.

My personal connection to hockey, rooted in my high school days when I shared classes with Edmonton Oil Kings players, made one assignment especially exciting. We were tasked with reimagining the management structure for the hit show "Hockey Night in Canada," the legendary joint venture between Molson Breweries and the CBC. This project allowed me to combine my professional expertise with my passion for the sport.

The opportunity to work on such a culturally significant program was both challenging and rewarding. "Hockey Night in Canada" wasn't just a television show; it was a national institution that brought Canadians together every Saturday night (and in the subsequent days), to debate and discuss the game highlights. Our work on restructuring its management had the potential to impact not only the program's operations but also its role in Canadian culture.

While working on Hockey Night in Canada (HNIC was its project name), I couldn't help but quietly hum, "When your tires are humming and your motor purrs, and your car is eager, and the thought occurs, that it's good to be alive in this land of ours . . ."

As consultants, we approached our report to middle management about the joint venture with a constructive and sunny disposition. The presentation took place in an intimate meeting room in Ottawa, around a table meant for six. The setting was compact yet focused, with two of us from Canada Consulting facing three CBC representatives. I had the privilege of leading the presentation, a responsibility that underscored the importance of our findings and recommendations. The close quarters of the room created an atmosphere of immediacy and engagement, allowing for direct communication and immediate feedback.

At the conclusion of the presentation, I sat down, and my consulting partner, seated across the table, asked if there were any questions. Suddenly, the CBC network executive to my left kicked me in the ankle as hard as he could and whispered something like "I don't want you here" in my ear. I was so shocked that all I could do was bend over slightly and gasp. No one seemed to notice, and when the meeting was over, I limped quietly out of the room.

Subsequently, my colleague remarked that he had only observed that I had gone rather quiet. "I guess he didn't like your report," he commented dryly. I suppose the executive couldn't kick me in the stomach without someone noticing.

I continued to work happily on what we described as "the assignments that came in over the transom while we were out marketing to the uninterested."

During the economic downturn of the early 1980s, I was involved in establishing the Ontario Centre for Automotive Parts Technology, which provided me with valuable insights into the intricacies of the automotive parts industry. This experience proved to be particularly relevant when Canada Consulting was subsequently engaged by the federal government to conduct a forward-looking study.

Our task was to examine the emergence of what we then called the "knowledge industry" and assess its potential impact on various economic sectors, with a particular focus on automobile manufacturing. This project was remarkably prescient, as it essentially explored concepts that we would now associate with the effects of artificial intelligence (AI) on traditional industries.

The study required us to envision how emerging technologies and information-based industries might reshape established manufacturing processes and business models. We analyzed potential disruptions, opportunities for innovation, and the changing skill requirements that might arise from this technological shift. Our work aimed to help policymakers and industry leaders prepare for the impending transformations in the automotive sector and beyond.

Looking back, this project was an early exploration of themes that have become central to discussions about Industry 4.0, smart manufacturing, and the digital transformation of traditional industries. It suggests that the seeds of today's AI revolution were already planted decades ago, and how forward-thinking analysis can help anticipate and shape technological transitions in key economic sectors.

CHAPTER FOURTEEN

Evolving

AS CANADA CONSULTING grew, we diversified our team by hiring more women, enriching our workplace with varied perspectives and talents. The firm buzzed with energy as each team member engaged in compelling projects across different sectors.

My own professional growth was evident. I had honed my skills in hypothesis testing and synthesis, developing a knack for distilling complex information into what the management consulting industry prizes: "clear, actionable insights." Indeed, my confidence in expressing opinions had also grown significantly. My newfound assertiveness didn't go unnoticed; after one particularly spirited company meeting, Neil quipped, "Do you eat with that tongue, Whittaker, or do you just shave with it?"

Some colleagues expressed concerns about my informal style with certain clients and my perceived lack of worry about my children. These observations highlighted the ongoing challenge of balancing professional demeanor with personal authenticity and managing work–life integration in a demanding career.

Despite these critiques and other minor missteps along the way, my contributions and growth trajectory were recognized. I achieved a significant milestone in my career by being promoted to partner at the firm. This advancement validated my approach and demonstrated that success could be had through a combination of skill, dedication, and a willingness to challenge conventional norms.

Our open office had three secretarial stations down the middle of the floor, which one would pass to go to or from our enclosed boardroom and the main door. Incidentally, we also had male and female single-seat washrooms tucked into the wall along the way. The toilets were plumbed back to back with very little insulation between them, so it was best to time your visits.

One day, as I was escorting a client out past the reception area, he casually referred to me as "Sweetie" and draped his arm around my shoulder. After he left, my secretary, who was known for her strong stance on professionalism, confronted me with a concerned expression. She asked, "Why did you let him treat you like that?"

I let out a sigh and smiled ruefully, recognizing the validity of her concern. I replied, "Sometimes in life, you just have to pick your battles." It was a moment that highlighted certain vexations of a gendered workplace, particularly when it comes to balancing assertiveness with diplomacy.

To be fair, everyone back then seemed to be struggling with sexist lexicons and finding ways to avoid terms like "man hours" as a measure of work. Even the term "chair" to replace "chairman" was stirring discomfort, provoking bad jokes and confusion. Just as today, I regularly check with my children to see if certain words, like "niggardly," meaning "stingy," which had never had a racist association, are still acceptable in modern parlance. (Answer: they are not.)

When Pierre Juneau assumed the presidency of the CBC in 1982, Canada Consulting was engaged to develop a strategic plan with him. Our firm was uniquely positioned for this task, given our extensive knowledge of the major issues and key players in the broadcasting industry. We swiftly prepared for our initial meetings with Juneau, armed with insights and ready to contribute to the CBC's future direction.

In our strategic discussions, we employed the widely used Boston Consulting Group's four-box matrix as a framework. Within this BCG matrix, we incorporated the term "unobtrusive" to describe a particular aspect of our strategy. Juneau, who was fully bilingual and deeply engaged in our sessions, took a keen interest in our presentation and the terminology we used.

Over the subsequent years of our professional relationship, I often found myself quietly amused whenever Juneau would use the word "unobstrusive" in discussions. Remarkably, this mispronunciation went uncorrected by others, and the term seemed to appear with surprising frequency in several of our conversations.

It wasn't until nearly fifteen years later, while reviewing old files, that I stumbled upon our original presentation document. To my shock and embarrassment, I discovered that I had inadvertently typed "unobstrusive" in the BCG matrix. This revelation cast our past interactions in a new light—what I had interpreted as Juneau's implicit acknowledgment of my expertise was, in fact, a faithful repetition of my typographical error.

Despite my earlier spelling oversight (in my defense, this was before the era of spellcheck), I later received a call from the senior vice-president of the CBC. He informed me that they were seeking to fill the position of Vice-President, Planning and Corporate Affairs.

The nature of this call didn't come as a surprise. The fact that the CBC sought my input for such a crucial position spoke volumes about the reputation Canada Consulting had built and the insights we were known to provide.

Gearing up, I began to discuss the position with the SVP. I suggested to him that the job would require someone with a unique blend of strategic thinking, industry knowledge, the energy to initiate change, and the ability to traverse the complex political landscape of public broadcasting, ideally both in English and in French.

I went on to assure the senior vice-president that I would carefully identify possible candidates and get back to him with my recommendations.

"No, Sheelagh," he said. "We were thinking about *you*."

"But I have a job and a family and live in Toronto, not Ottawa," I replied.

"Maybe you could commute," he suggested. "I commute from Montreal."

I was shocked and flattered, but Mike was supportive, and Canada Consulting was supportive, and CCG entered into a kind of lend-lease deal where I commuted to Ottawa for two years and then would return to my responsibilities in Toronto. As I used to describe it, on Mondays I would take an early flight and eat the airline breakfast and on Fridays I would return, drinking the airline's white wine.

The job was both exhilarating and exhausting. There were no guard rails on my working hours, so I would often work until the Toronto Blue Jays were in their third inning. Sometimes the kids came to stay with me in my pied-à-terre in Ottawa or the family would all come up for the weekend.

Midway through my tenure, our family faced a significant change when my sister Terree made the difficult decision that she could no longer raise her second child, Daniel, who was just 22 months old at the time. This situation was not entirely unfamiliar to us, as my older sister Penny had previously adopted Terree's first child, making the concept of adoption a part of our family's narrative. From the moment Daniel joined Mike's and my family, we were all smitten.

In 1986, the Canadian broadcasting landscape was evolving rapidly, with specialty channels emerging as a new frontier for cable broadcasters. Recognizing this shift, the Canadian Radio-television and Telecommunications Commission (CRTC) issued a call for competitive applications from both public and private sectors for a license to operate a specialty news channel.

This initiative presented a significant opportunity for the CBC, and it became a focal point of my work there. Collaborating closely with the News and Current Affairs department, I played a key role in developing and presenting our application for what would become Newsworld, now known as CBC News Network. This project was particularly exciting as it represented a major expansion of CBC's news coverage capabilities and its ability to serve Canadians with round-the-clock news programming.

Our efforts were ultimately successful, marking a pivotal moment in Canadian broadcasting history. The launch of Newsworld not only enhanced CBC's news offerings but also set a new standard for 24-hour news coverage in Canada.

While working on signature projects like Newsworld, I also focused on addressing nuanced aspects of broadcasting policy. One such initiative involved lobbying for a change in advertising regulations to allow for the promotion of feminine hygiene products on CBC Television. This effort, which might have once seemed less glamorous than launching a new channel, was important in modernizing CBC's advertising policies and reflecting changing societal norms.

In the broader business world, while at CBC, I was invited to join the board of Sterling Trust Co., an Ontario-based company. As was often the case in my life, I was both flattered and confused. I checked with both Canada Consulting and CBC, and they saw no reason for me to refuse, so I accepted. And what a charming bunch the Sterling Trust directors were. Mostly Scottish-Canadians in the tradition of trust companies, and very punctilious. I was honored to be part of their organization.

Was that, I wonder, the first real glass shard I'd chipped away? Certainly, I was not unique in terms of women then sitting on corporate boards, but was my route to that position novel? There must have been a headhunter involved, as I knew no one in that organization before my selection. But why me?

Around that time, Mike had a very likable and smart female colleague who had a similarly accomplished mother, albeit her personality turned some people away. The mother, daughter, Mike, and I were having drinks together one evening when she started pontificating about how, while she held a board position in an esteemed charitable organization, it should be quite a while before women were selected for "serious" corporate boards for fear they had insufficient experience or competence in such matters.

Subsequently, Mike reminded me that it was during this conversation that I first declared, somewhat stridently, "We will have true equality when we have as many incompetent women in positions of power as we have incompetent men."

Over the years, some of my best friendships have evolved from people who came looking for the woman (me) who was recorded in Colombo's Canadian Quotations for having first said that.

Recently, I encountered an August 2022 article in the *Harvard Business Review* entitled "Why Do So Many Incompetent Men Become Leaders?" by T. Chamorro-Premuzic. He concludes: "In sum, there is no denying that women's path to leadership positions is paved with many barriers, including a very thick glass ceiling. But a much greater problem is the lack of career obstacles for incompetent men, and the fact that we tend to equate leadership with the very psychological features that make the average man a more inept leader than the average woman."

Looking at women in politics and business these days, I'd say both genders may be moving toward the mean.

CHAPTER FIFTEEN

The Kids Are All Right

ONE DAY IN the late 1980s, after a pleasant business lunch where we had touched on a wide range of current business and political issues, a senior political advisor asked me, "So, what do your kids do while you are off working?"

Shocked, I replied, "They get older. They go to school, and they read books, and they play sports and they play Nintendo. They are nice kids who get good grades and think their nanny smokes too much and looks like Boy George. I do, too, but she makes sure that she smokes outside, and good nannies are hard to get."

He had the decency to be embarrassed.

The quality of childcare you provide is inevitably shaped by your own experiences. One of my sister Penny's fondest memories is of me, dressed in a stunning floor-length white wedding gown with a train, picking up lint from the carpet at the foot of the stairs in our Edmonton home. She recognized, even if I didn't at the time, that the carpet would soon be covered in confetti. I likely would have done it anyway, driven by a sense of duty and care.

In an early pre-children dwelling, I was fortunate to have a beautiful stainless steel refrigerator—one of the first of its kind. Being a bit neurotic about spots and stains (I'm never without my magic sponge), I realized I was spending what felt like a disproportionate amount of time shining the refrigerator doors.

I remember sitting at the slick-wiped kitchen table, thinking, "This isn't what I want my life to be—shining fridge doors and telling kids to go play in another room. I don't want to be the one worrying about the mess rather than being known as the relaxed enabler of remarkable finger painting. But it's really not in my neurotic soul to be otherwise."

So I ducked that role, and, apart from coming in the door each evening and saying "Please don't hug mommy until she has her work clothes off," it has all worked out for the best. (Dry cleaning was expensive in those days.)

I felt honored when my 30-year-old Meghan told me that I was a "good mother for adults." As I said to my daughter then, "You're an adult for a lot longer than you're a child, so if you get to pick—and not everybody does—pick the good adult version."

She also told me that she still uses the same dry cleaner on Parliament Street in Toronto that I used forty years ago, and that the dry cleaner had told her recently that he still remembers her mother: "a statuesque woman with a taste for silk blouses."

CHAPTER SIXTEEN

The Days Mommy Got Angry

ANGER IS NOT an emotion I experience often. In fact, in my family, only the older kids, Meghan and Matthew, and their dad remember a day when mommy got angry. My long-ago Canada Consulting Group colleague, Madeleine, probably still recalls an incident at work. And my sister Penny claims I used to bite her when I was little and felt thwarted, but the marks have finally faded, so she has no proof.

This particular day was stressful from the start. I had been on the stand as a consultant and expert witness in the "Family Griddle with Warmer" civil damages case, and the plaintiff's lawyers had failed to finish their cross-examination. The central challenge in the case was determining the potential sales volume of the competitor's similar products, had they not been barred from the market pending the resolution of the copyright infringement dispute. My background in anti-trust made it a natural fit for me, but cross-examination is very stressful.

The court was now in recess, set to resume in ten days. Meanwhile, Mike and I were scheduled to fly at dawn the next day to a newly developed tourist destination in Venezuela, and I hadn't yet packed. For some alcohol-related reason, dinner time had come and gone, and Mike had yet to arrive home. I was watching *The Dukes of Hazzard* on the sofa upstairs with Matt and Meghan.

Finally, I heard him enter the front door and traverse the main floor through the living and dining area to the kitchen. I hurried downstairs to greet him and discovered, as I approached the bottom of our open staircase, that he had unknowingly stepped on dog poo on his way home. He had just tracked it liberally across the light beige wall-to-wall carpet on our main floor.

Angrily, I pushed past him to get my cleaning products and begin tackling the filthy carpet. Mike stood by ineffectually and suggested that it was lucky the carpet was beige.

I don't remember many more details, just that I shouted at Mike to take his shoes off, and that Matthew, timid in those days, retreated upstairs to the television. Meghan, slowly climbing backward up the open staircase, said, "Oh, Mommy, please don't get more angry," and I said, in a stentorian tone, "It would be impossible for me to be any angrier than I am right now." And I think that remains true to this day.

Mike left the building and came home again much later.

By the way, we caught the plane to Venezuela and it was a really remarkable and fun vacation. Venezuela was trying to figure out how to become a tourist destination and everyone was trying very hard to make us want to come back.

Recalling another of my rare though memorable bouts of anger, my son Matthew tells me that he likes the story of "The Day Mommy Stamped Her Foot."

It was around 1 p.m. on the Friday before the Monday due date for the Cantel applications, and I was at work. I had just spoken to the manager of the French translators, who informed me that the translators were crying with fatigue at their typewriters. An unfair aspect of Canada's policy of bilingualism in those days was that the translators usually received the final copy to work on only after everyone on the English side was done.

I was talking to the office manager, Madeleine, who oversaw the site we had rented to accomplish our task. The consultant in charge of printing and collating final versions approached me and reported that we had accumulated roughly sixty-five hours of printing on all the machines, but we only had around five hours left before the copy shop we had engaged was scheduled to close.

I stamped my foot. Hard.

Suddenly, I felt untethered from my body, as if I were on the ceiling, looking down at this ridiculous woman with tangled hair who had just stamped her foot in the face of appalling news. And then my brain switched into gear.

"There is requisite duplication in the submissions for the various territories we are applying for, so let's pull out all the duplicate sections, like engineering specifications and radio and TV advertising, and photocopy them while the other parts are printing. Then we can reinsert them into the regional masters," I said. "And call the copy shop and tell them we will need them to stay late. Really late as it turned out.

My foot-stamping worked!

There was a lot of lore around that project, like the advertising executive who handed me the bill for our breakfast at the King George Hotel after I had just given him the entire creative job and told him we needed the mockups by 7 a.m. the next day, or the surprisingly patient girlfriends of the photocopy guys who finally gave up on their dates and went home alone at 3 a.m. on Sunday.

But it turns out, anger isn't really my thing. I'm a "take the high road" kind of person, and I think it has stood me in good stead as I barged along, looking for the elevator that would take me to the level where you get to walk out and saunter with gaiety atop the glass floor, trying not to look down.

CHAPTER SEVENTEEN

Being a Witness Seems to Run in the Family

I SHOULD EXPLAIN THE omnipresence of the name "Whittaker" strewn throughout this book. When Meghan was born, we registered her as Meghan Whittaker-Van Dusen. However, while I was at home with her in married students' housing, I received a call from a laid-back Ontario government representative who said, "Lady, we don't do hyphens." So, we compromised and registered her as Meghan Whittaker (middle name) Van Dusen.

When Mike returned home, he and I agreed not to tell anyone about the "hyphens" call and to simply use Meg's name as hyphenated. We did the same with Matthew.

Privately, I cited as my authority on this matter a telephone call I overheard in 1965. The call involved Ivan Head, who was then a faculty member at the University of Alberta law school. Head, who later became a Canadian diplomat, gave the opinion to a caller that "a person's name is whatever they choose to call themselves."

Thinking back, I was in Ivan Head's office because he was a family friend, and I was asking for his help on an essay about Emily Murphy for my Canadian History course. Emily Murphy was one of the "Famous Five," women who had won the right in 1929 for women to be legally considered "persons" under Canadian law, specifically for the purpose of being appointed to the Senate. This victory came just two months before my "greatest generation" representative Merrijoy Kelner was born.

In fact, the Supreme Court of Canada had initially ruled against the women in 1928, declaring that women were not "persons" under the British North America Act. The Famous Five then appealed to the Judicial Committee of the Privy Council in Britain, at that time Canada's highest court of appeal. On October 18, 1929, the Privy Council overturned the Supreme Court's decision, thereby establishing women's right to be considered "persons" under Canadian law.

By the time we adopted Daniel, Ontario allowed hyphens.

I received several strange calls during the three months we lived, unmarried, in York University's married students' housing. One sunny morning, a branch of the Government of Canada called to give me a pre-employment bilingualism test for my Combines job. I asked them to call back in fifteen minutes so I could get dressed and put in my contact lenses. It's hard to speak French on the phone in your muumuu without your glasses.

I think our son Matthew discovered our clever ruse when applying for his passport at sixteen, and he was not pleased about having had to spell out his mildly confusing name for all those years. His solution was to drop the "Whittaker" in everyday usage. Meghan tried to resolve the dilemma by getting married and becoming simply Meghan Scott, but the registrar told her she had to be Meghan Whittaker Scott because her legal middle name is Whittaker. So, she named her children Turner Whittaker Scott and Alexandra Whittaker Scott. As he matured, Turner noticed that his father's middle name was not Whittaker and asked why his dad was not the same as the rest of the family. I don't know what Turner's dad told him. Meghan is now married to a Donaldson, but her career has been in the name of Scott, and she fears the outcome if she tries to change it.

My last child is called Nicholas Whittaker Morgan, but the reader hasn't really met his dad yet, and he was not the type to countenance a hyphen.

With that probably unnecessary amount of detail (although there is a lot more where that came from), here is the experience of a child of a woman who kind of lived by feminist principles:

"Insights from a Representative of Generation X"

By Meghan Whittaker Scott, LLD

When you're little, you think that however your world is, that's how the whole world is. So if you grow up in a nice semi-detached home on a cute street in a Victorian neighborhood downtown, that's how everyone's house is.

If your parents did their MBA degree together, and they say things to you and your brothers, like "We will pay for your first university degree, but you have to pay for your second degree," that's the plan for every kid.

If your house is governed by a young British nanny with a pack-a-day cigarette habit, who runs the house with lots of rules and an unpredictable temper, then that's how everyone's nanny is.

If you grow up with both parents going to work every day and coming home from work around six p.m. to a stiff scotch and dinner with the kids, that's what everyone's parents do after a long day of work.

And then one day, you realize that the world isn't the same for everyone.

Perhaps your eyes are opened by reading tons of books all the time. Everything from Holocaust survivors' writings to Sweet Valley High. Or perhaps you are surprised by the friend who comes over for a party and says "You live here? Like, this whole house is just for your family?" Or maybe it's later when the single mother of your friend asks your parents if your nanny could watch her daughter on the PD day, because she has no child care if there's no school that day.

Maybe it's when your mother takes a job in a city five hours away by car, because "CBC Vice President, Planning and Corporate Affairs" is too big an opportunity to pass up. Most people's moms aren't only home on the weekends.

Regardless of how it happens, eventually you become aware that the world outside your front door doesn't actually mirror the world inside your house.

When you watch *Charlie's Angels* at night, you say to your mom, who is packing for the next week in her closet near the TV, that you want to be a Charlie's angel when you grow up. That prompts her to stop what she's doing to say, "a Charlie's angel isn't a real job. But you know what is a job for cool girls fighting crime? Being a prosecutor. You still get to get the bad guys, but you're a lawyer instead."

And that was it. At age ten, you write an essay for school about how you plan to be a prosecutor one day. You will go to school, get good grades, go to university for your first degree, paid for by parents, then to law school, paid for by yourself. You don't remember the essay, but your mother does. And she sits back and watches, pleased, while you make the essay come true. You don't need a whole lot of help with this plan. You're the eldest. And a girl. You can do anything.

In high school you make progress. You aren't cool, exactly, but you have a group of close friends. And those friends, who come from various types of families, all have one thing in common: all their moms work. All their moms are smart, well-read, interesting women, all of whom raised their daughters to be that way, too.

Your friends are generally outgoing, and not afraid to be smart out loud. Sometimes during lunch, they get into arguments over what a word means, or how to pronounce something. One will insist that she knows best because her mother is a nurse. The other will respond by saying she's right because her mother is an editor. All of you vie for attention from the English teacher, who tells your parents, "Meghan is incisive." Well, you were right to announce to the class that Holden Caulfield *was* a loser, and your boldness in doing so only underscores your teacher's assessment of your incisive nature.

Your girlfriends all have big plans for their lives: lawyers (two), journalists (two), writers (several), a Hollywood actor, a professor, a headhunter. Yeah, you all plan to get married and have kids, but that's the backdrop, not the main event, in our future selves. You go to different universities, and take different paths to our careers, but always stay close.

University is fun. You were ready to be adults.

Law school is a bit less fun. For one thing, you are far away from home and a little bit lonely.

But then you get involved in student politics: as first-year rep to the Law Students' Association (LSA), then Vice President Internal, then in third year, President. And the cherry on top was getting elected valedictorian and delivering a speech to the graduating class.

You finally move home. Your mom, who has been running the Canadian operations of an international technology services firm for the past many years has decided to take a position with the same company in Australia, where your stepfather was born. They move there shortly after you come home, taking your eight-year old baby brother with them.

You're a career woman now, with a demanding Bay Street job that prompted you to relocate from the West Coast to Toronto. Your boyfriend reluctantly followed, understanding the importance of your career. Early in your relationship, he paid you an unconventional compliment, saying he admired "bitches who get shit done." While his choice of words was crude, you understood the sentiment behind it; he values your drive and competence.

Up to this point, you have had a somewhat Pollyannaish view of the world, at least as it relates to women in positions of power. You took over the Law Students' Association presidency from another girl. That girl being former Chief Justice of the Supreme Court of Canada, Beverley McLachlin. Your law school class was about 51:49 women to men. You get an articling position at the largest law firm in Canada, and the majority of the twenty-five articling students in your year are women. Girls can do anything. It's never occurred to you to challenge that assertion.

You and your boyfriend end up working a few blocks apart as articling students. You keep the same bananas hours. You occasionally meet for dinner in the food court under your office tower and then go back to work. He comes to Thursday drinks with your fellow articling students at the super fancy resto at the top of your tower. You drink amaretto sours. You all feel like titans of industry. Okay, like titans in training. At the end of your articling year, you get placed in the litigation section.

You get pregnant at the end of your first year as a lawyer, finding out mere days before your wedding. This is working out perfectly. At age twenty-four, you had told your then boyfriend that you were on a five-year plan for marriage and children. He had requested that the plan be extended to ten years for children. You had declined his counteroffer. Now, at the four-year mark, you have already achieved the plan's stated goals. Is there a performance bonus for doing it early?

You take maternity leave for a total of seven months. Four paid months, then you use up all your vacation and you go without a salary for a bit. You transition from you at home with baby to a leave/family vacation with a husband at home and a baby for a month. That was a novel idea when he did it. People always commented on how unusual it was for a dad to stay home with the baby. He was a good dad, and his boss was ahead of his time. You're lucky, although sad, to leave your baby at home.

When you get back to work, everything has changed. There is now someone whom you want to rush home to every day. You miss out on the evening of continuing legal education sessions they hold about once a month. You send an email to the people in charge to let them know that you could make it if they ran the sessions over breakfast or lunch but that by 6:30 p.m. you need to be home with the baby. They don't reply to your email.

You have your first review post-mat leave. They tell you that they have been made aware that you have not been attending the education sessions at night. They tell you that you should get a nighttime nanny so you can stay at work later. You bravely resist the urge to say that you didn't have a child you would never see. But when you leave that room, you start looking for a new job. You went to school to be a prosecutor. Go do it.

You are supremely lucky and, within a few months, get a contract with the prosecutor's office. It's a dramatic pay cut, and it's a short-term contract, with no guarantee of permanency. But it's what you've always wanted to do. When the boss offers you that job, you say, "I don't want you to feel that I took this job under false pretenses. I'm pregnant." He says that's not a problem, so long as you know that you won't get any benefits from the contract position while on mat leave. You don't care. You are so damn happy to have this job, you take it. Not incidentally, when you look back at the people hired by the boss over the many years he held that position, you realize he hired exclusively smart young women as articling students and prosecutors every single time. One of his three deputies was a woman. The office was more than 50 percent women for years.

You love that job. You love the parry and thrust of being in court every day. You love the collegiality of an office where no one worries about billable hours or making partner. You love the fact that the work you're doing has a real-life positive impact on victims of crime, on accused persons and, more broadly, on society as a whole. You even love that you're crammed into small, windowless rooms in a bunker of a courthouse, even though that courthouse sometimes has bedbugs and the population that attends at that courthouse sometimes hasn't washed in days. It's real life, it's real law, and you quickly make friends with a group of women who really get you: they understand the ridiculous things that happen in court, the judges who yell at you, the people who lie to you. They share your dark sense of humor. They look like ladies, but they talk like pirates.

Sometimes you take your mother to work with you when she's in town. She has always loved reading "evil but true" stories, as she called them, or true crime novels, as most others do. She loved sitting in court until the judge would say, "Ma'am, do you have a matter here today?" and then she would say, "Oh no, I'm the prosecutor's mother. It's take-your-mommy to work day." One time, when prosecuting an especially challenging HIV sex assault jury trial with very fragile victims, your mom mothered them, offering them words of support during their panic attacks and money for food when they had none. She calls herself their fairy godmother. The victim turned to her and he said, "Usually they call me the fairy." We all laughed. She is very interested in your cases. She still remembers the details of some of them years later. She's proud of you, too, and she will tell anyone and everyone she's your mother. "Mom!" you say when you find her talking to random people, "That's an accused person!" "Oh," she says, "he seemed nice. He agreed with me that you were very good at your job." Her beloved older sister was a lawyer. That sister's middle daughter is a lawyer. In your family, for whatever reason, the lawyers are all women.

Time marches on. And you, always ambitious, apply to be deputy prosecutor after a few years. You don't get it the first time you apply. Admittedly, it's a stretch. You're still pretty junior. The female boss who took over from the boss who hired you is amazing. She tells you that even though you didn't get it this time, you will next time. She is supportive of everyone in the office. She takes you out when you are wrongly accused of abusing process, this being a serious charge hurled at you by a defendant's counsel, suggesting you've used legal procedures for an improper purpose or to harass and pressure a defendant, rather than to pursue justice. She buys you a cup of hot chocolate because you don't drink coffee, and she says, "In this line of work, if no one is accusing you of abusing process or suing you, you're probably not doing the job properly." You adore her. But after six years, she leaves the office.

In the meantime, you fall in love with a woman. It's a bit of a surprise to you, and to your husband. But the love is mutual, and it's overwhelming. Everyone leaves their present spouse and gets remarried. Your new spouse is a police officer who works in a very male-dominated world, and she's a very physical one. She is one tough cookie, as one might imagine from someone who has climbed so high within a paramilitary organization. Oddly, while sexism certainly exists in her workplace, the police have been increasingly clear about prioritizing the promotion of women and people of color within the organization. She deals with some creeps, to be sure, but she's never had a boss who overtly prioritizes men for perks or promotions.

Back to the prosecution service. The person who takes over from the girl boss in your office is a man from another office. He's not a creep. He doesn't harass any of the women. He just clearly isn't that comfortable around them. He is awkward, and he routinely says things that make people uncomfortable. There are complaints about him. He does not change. But the atmosphere in the office changes. The people who once loved their jobs stopped loving them. The ambitious group of women you hang around with have been largely stuck at their existing ranks. Over the ensuing nine years, there is one promotion of a female. And then, you're briefly given an acting deputy role. Eighteen years on the job, and you're finally moving up! You work your butt off, and people seem to like you. Even the boss suggests that he thinks you're doing a good job. But the man who was preferred for the role becomes available, and you are quickly relieved of your acting role.

Nothing stays the same forever. Your office is relocated to a large downtown courthouse, and the small offices that once existed throughout the city are merged and reconstituted into this single location. The result is startling: out of sixteen bosses and deputies, there is only one female boss, and just three other women are designated as leaders. In the year 2023, you wonder, couldn't they find more women to put on the leadership teams of offices that are predominantly staffed by women? You and your female colleagues openly question how the optics of such an imbalance don't seem to concern those in higher positions.

Your new team recently had a deputy competition. You apply, of course. You always do. When one of the bosses who conducted the interviews came in to tell you that you didn't get it, he was complimentary. He said, "You're a lot like me. I bet you've never been on a volunteer organization that you didn't ultimately end up running." It was a funny thing to say, in part because it was true. He went on to say, "I'm sure you're demoralized about not getting it, but don't give up. You're on our radar now, and we will keep you in mind for future leadership opportunities." You thanked him, and then, because you're bold like this, you said, "I note that on your leadership team, you have no female deputies. Perhaps you'd like to put me in a leadership role on your team?" He laughed at your suggestion.

In a world filled with generations of strong, powerful, and accomplished women, things are still not equal. Even when you are a smart, assertive woman, you hit the glass ceiling repeatedly. Maybe you're too assertive? Who knows? Regardless, you hope that your beautiful, funny, unbelievably smart daughter, who just started studying Engineering at university, will experience a world that is less sexist and more equal than your own experience in the workplace.

But when she comes home for her first Reading Week in November, she says, "You kept telling me before I went away, 'You will be fine in a course with a bunch of guys because you're a tough cookie,' and I thought you were exaggerating about how few girls there would be. But when I got to school and saw that in my block of forty-five, there were only four girls, I realized I was delusional."

And that's when it hits you: anyone who believes we have achieved equality in the workplace is delusional. As your mother, the wildly successful business executive, used to say when asked about equality in the workplace, "We won't achieve full equality until there are as many incompetent women in positions of power as there are men." And right now, even competent women are not in positions of power in equal numbers. We are a long way from equality.

Thank you, Meghan. I agree.—Mom

CHAPTER EIGHTEEN

Proceeding along as a Non-Linear Thinker

I AM SOMEWHAT ANTI-SYSTEMATIC. I struggle with simple ordering principles and am poor at distinguishing right from left and North/ South/ East/ West. When I had to write, "I will not talk in class" one hundred times, as I often did in grade school, I would start with 100 vertical "I"s, then move to 90 "wills," then 73 "nots," and, finally, 82 "talks." Or the ink color might vary. Sometimes I eat dessert first, or I make my bed in stages throughout the day. You get the picture.

As I look up from my writing, I see the beautiful needlepoint Penny crafted and gave to me while she was juggling her career as a lawyer and raising her children. It features pink flowers adorning the sides and across the top, with blue letters arranged in uppercase from A to Z, below which are the numbers 1 to 8.

Recently, I discovered an unfinished needlework of my own in a neglected drawer, likely inspired by Penny's gift. I vividly recall the last time I worked on it: I was on Varadero Beach in Cuba, and Matthew was due to be born soon, so it must have been around February 1977. My needlework has decorative elements completed around the top and sides, with the letters A to X executed in blue thread.

Nature or nurture?

After my stint as a vice-president at CBC, the broadcaster wanted me to stay on, and I kind of wanted to as well, but I was afraid that the VP position might be "about it," and family and Canada Consulting were calling me back to Toronto.

Ed Sexton, my esteemed lawyer friend from a major Combines case, had accidentally discovered, while sitting beside me on the Ottawa–Toronto air shuttle, that I had inadvertently retained one of law firm Osler, Hoskin & Harcourt's large legal briefcases from our time prosecuting Hoffman-La Roche for predatory pricing. He was dismayed because he had vouched for my character to the firm. Ed insisted I return it.

This revelation presented a dilemma. How could I continue my frequent commutes without a capacious, official-looking bag to store my papers and personal items? Nonetheless, I agreed. The law firm was understandably surprised to receive the document bag back after so many years.

Around this time, my son Matthew, age eleven, completed a school project called "Life's Been Good to Me So Far." It is both smart and touching. In his description of "My Family," he writes about me:

> When she was twenty-nine, she made the biggest mistake of her life, she had my sister. Then she made up for that mistake, she had me. She got a job at Canada Consulting after college. Then, after four or five years of working there, she moved to CBC and became Vice President fourth in charge of the whole system. Then she moved back to Canada Consulting just to move to Cancom, a communications company. But through all this she has stayed the same and I still love my 'mommis.'

I was very pleased to be back in the bosom of my family. The kids were flourishing, and Mike was enjoying his work environment at Hewlett Packard. I fit right back into the joys of marketing while I waited for the unexpected assignment to come in over the transom. Fortunately, CCG had saved my desk and chair.

As Matthew had observed, a few months later I was asked out for coffee by Pierre Morrissette, a good friend from what I privately referred to as the Cantel-application boot camp. Pierre was now CEO of Canadian Satellite Communications, Inc. The purpose of his invitation to meet was simple: he wanted me to join his firm as Chief Financial Officer.

I had imagined myself in a few different executive positions, but never CFO. But as Pierre reassured me, he was a qualified CFO and I had an educational background in finance, economics, legal analysis and administration, an MBA, consulting experience, and a questionable mastery of French, plus he knew I could do the job. In addition, he added, it wouldn't be for long as he had another, more senior post in mind, but right now what he needed was a CFO. He also reassured me that he would never be far away when complex financial decisions were to be made.

Around this time, I began to describe my career path as "incremental opportunism." I was going along happily doing whatever it was that I was doing, and some opportunity would materialize out of left field, usually a job that I would never have put myself forward for, and I would take it. I mean, what was the worst that could happen to me, other than being declared surplus to needs? And if that happened, I felt confident I'd just keep going.

One constraint I was unaware of at that time, and just as well, is the Law of Accumulated Exposure. I was only forty-one years old and had only been strutting my time upon the boards in a conspicuous way for about a decade, and I was still considered to be a kid. Those who didn't like me were reduced to leaking falsehoods about me to the press or taking credit for my ideas. Lots of people either hadn't yet met me or still liked me. It would take a while before my irreverent laugh and my sometimes divergent points of view attracted enough exposure to make me vincible.

Unfortunately, on the home front, Mike and I had run up against the Law of Accumulated Exposure and amicably agreed to go our separate romantic ways. While we tried to keep things as no-fault as possible, the kids' distress was still our fault.

CHAPTER NINETEEN

Beaming Up

I HAD COMPLETED SEVERAL consulting projects for the cable industry while at Canada Consulting, and I knew many of the players—and liked most of them. However, the inner workings of Canadian Satellite Communications (Cancom) were new to me. I remember with gratitude how patient and thoughtful my new staff were during those early months.

We were in the business of "doing good" by providing TV channels by satellite to remote and underserved communities in Canada, which otherwise might only have access to CBC or CBC and CTV. As my son Daniel once queried, "Why are they called 'undeserved'?" (I quickly corrected his misunderstanding.) We also provided signals to direct-to-home satellite dishes and business networks and were investigating new satellite-enabled businesses. Additionally, we had the beginnings of a medical health network and were trying to develop efficient educational networks, long before COVID-19.

Mercifully, after only one annual general meeting answering questions as CFO, I was promoted to Executive Vice President, and my much better qualified assistant CFO, Louise, took my place. The VP of Corporate Affairs was Susan, which now put Cancom at the forefront of executive gender equality. We also had a VP in charge of Indigenous Affairs who was Indigenous. Sadly, he died not long after I arrived.

I loved my work. Pierre Morrissette was a joy to work with, and my office, adjacent to his, offered a panoramic view of Mississauga. As a company regulated by the CRTC with an array of small leading-edge suppliers, the work was always challenging and dynamic. Our profitability improved steadily under Pierre's leadership.

It wasn't long before Pierre took me aside and shared his plans to leave the company to establish his own venture, Pelmorex Media Inc. He said he would recommend to the board of directors at their next meeting that I be appointed CEO in his place. Pierre expressed confidence that with this appointment, he would be leaving the company in capable hands.

Pierre conveyed this to the board as well. Cancom had a very strong board of seasoned executives from across Canada, carefully chosen to ensure non-executive coverage of our vast target market. Chairperson Ray Peters was an experienced chair, friend, and supporter. I was told later that Frank A. Griffiths, founder of Western International Communications and the major shareholder of Cancom, closed off a lively discussion of possible alternatives and my strengths and weaknesses by saying, "I think Sheelagh should have it."

And that was that.

While the board was meeting to discuss the CEO position, I found myself at loose ends and went shopping, purchasing a rather fetching pink linen suit with a matching silk blouse. Upon returning home, William, now my live-in partner, informed me that Ray Peters had been desperately trying to reach me. (This was before the era of mandatory mobile phones for executives.)

I had met William at the CBC where we had collaborated on managing the licensing of Newsworld, the 24-hour news channel. We were inordinately proud of that accomplishment, which had strengthened both our professional bond and personal relationship.

I promptly returned Ray Peters' call, and he inquired about my whereabouts. "Dealing with tension," I answered candidly. He then informed me that I had been appointed CEO of Canadian Satellite Communications, Inc. My newly purchased pink linen suit and silk blouse lay by the door, momentarily forgotten in light of this news. To my recollection, the stock market adopted a 'wait and see' attitude toward this leadership change.

That Christmas, I received a T-shirt from William emblazoned with "When the going gets tough, the tough go shopping."

CHAPTER TWENTY

Games Your Mother Couldn't Teach You

NOT LONG BEFORE that life-changing promotion, I read a very insightful book called *Games Your Mother Never Taught You: Corporate Gamesmanship for Women* by Betty Lehan Harragan, published in 1978. To me, it was a well-written, often humorous, guide to understanding and navigating behavior in the male-dominated world of commerce. Harragan's work was groundbreaking for its time, offering practical advice for women entering corporate environments that were still largely unfamiliar territory.

In the context of women's liberation, Betty Harragan realized that one significant difference in the upbringing of males and females was that the prevailing syllabus for the education of girls did not place much emphasis on the rough-and-tumble fellowship of team sports. Girls generally were not encouraged to play intramural sports, share showers, or go for drinks afterward.

While we in Western Canada had the world champion Edmonton Grads to be proud of, that was only one women's basketball team, and they rose to fame in the 1920s, playing until 1940. They stopped in 1940 at the beginning of the Second World War, when their arena was taken over to be used as a military manning depot.

I took brief exception to the term "manning depot," but when I looked it up online, I found that it was indeed the correct designation. The Internet clearly confirmed that "trainees began their military careers at a Manning Depot, where they learned to bathe, shave, shine boots, polish buttons, maintain their uniforms, and otherwise conduct themselves in the required manner." This led me to wonder if that is where the phrase "man up" originated.

Harragan's book made me think about the approach to a task one might observe from a man who competed enthusiastically in athletics versus a woman who spent her time reading novels or swimming solo. This helped me recognize that there were likely notable differences.

The first hurdle I remember encountering was my choice of office. I had settled into a comfortable, sunny office next to that of the former CEO, Pierre, and I was inclined to keep it and let the new EVP move into the corner office. Suddenly, a large piece of glass fell from the ceiling in the hall between both office doors, hit me on the head, and rendered me semi-conscious.

"CEOs work in CEOs' offices," a voice that might have been Betty Harragan's whispered to me, and I listened. Then I crawled over to the rope ladder that had descended from the ceiling when the piece of glass fell out and I shimmied up it. Then, again crawling, I moved cautiously across the rather thick glass floor. As I looked down at my hardworking colleagues through the glass, relieved to find it was one-way glass since my skirt was rather short, I was reminded of one of my favorite quotations from Shakespeare's *Julius Caesar*:

> *Why, man, he does bestride the narrow world*
> *Like a Colossus, and we petty men*
> *Walk under his huge legs and peep about*
> *To find ourselves dishonourable graves.*
> *Men at some time are masters of their fates:*
> *The fault, dear Brutus, is not in our stars*
> *But in ourselves that we are underlings.*
> —Act 1, Scene 2

When I recovered my senses, I discovered I was sitting in the luxurious leather swivel desk chair in my new office, and my assistant was asking me if I wanted to have a bowl of potpourri in the executive washroom.

Thinking about Harragan's book today, I realize that the title is incorrect. The problem did not arise because mothers withheld or failed to pass on information or experience to their daughters; they simply didn't have access to the female equivalent of any manning depots. They didn't know what they needed to teach us.

The title for the book should be *Games Your Mother Couldn't Teach You: Corporate Gamesmanship for Women.*

On April 19, 1989, Cancom Chairperson Ray Peters announced my appointment as the Company's President and Chief Executive Officer, promoting me from my previous role as Executive Vice President. The following month, I was featured on the cover of *Cablecaster Magazine*, standing in a bright red jacket, positioned in front of Len, our VP in charge of sales to cable companies. The accompanying article highlighted Cancom's newly achieved profitability.

This appointment marked a historic moment, as I became the first female CEO of a company listed on the Toronto Stock Exchange. Like most new senior executives, I was initially riding on the momentum generated by the company's energetic and innovative team and the performance of my predecessor. However, I was acutely aware that it was now my responsibility to maintain and accelerate the business's growth trajectory.

We had a lot of fun. Yet again, I found myself in an organization where, in this case, the engineers thought that the singular of "premises" was "premise." We dealt with land and buildings all the time. They also didn't understand why some of us giggled in meetings when they talked about how many "non-penetrating roof mounts" they were going to use for a particular installation. Just as well.

The business steadily grew.

The boardroom table in our conference room near the reception area could seat twelve, and the receptionist claimed she could hear laughter and even beautiful singing emanating from the room during meetings. (The VP of Corporate Affairs was the granddaughter of an acclaimed professional soprano.)

On a "take your child to work Saturday because you have nowhere else to leave him" day, my son Daniel was coloring in the boardroom while I was doing something or other. When I came to get him, he asked, "Mom, where do you sit when you have meetings? Do you sit here at the top of the table where I am sitting?"

"No, Dan," I replied ruefully, "I sit here at the middle facing the double doors."

"But you're the boss, you should sit where bosses sit."

"It's my instinct, Dan. I sit here facing the doors so that when a disgruntled customer with a machine gun breaks in, I'll be the first to spot him."

"Oh," Dan thought for a little, "Can I have a sausage with mustard from the guy on the street for lunch?"

"Yes. I want one too. Let's go."

Early in the 1990s, the *Toronto Star* ran an article entitled "Female Managers—Companies Keep Some, Lose Many," which lamented the slow progress of women through the corporate ranks, advancing the position that "breaking the glass ceiling, however, is easier said than done. The problem resides in the minds of senior male managers and supervisors."

In that article, my name and photo were paired with two other women with the concession that "some women have prospered in the 1980s."

Back at Cancom, new channels like Newsworld had been added to the Cancom package, and initiatives such as truck-tracking and messaging were progressing well. Consequently, the Board was pleased with these developments.

Out of the blue, we were offered a fascinating opportunity to work with Glavkosmos, originally established as part of the USSR's space program. The plan, tacitly supported by the Canadian government, was to jointly launch and operate a commercial satellite. The USSR (and later Russia) had geostationary orbit positions to spare and extensive experience in launching and operating spacecraft, while Cancom had expertise in using satellites for commercial purposes.

Glavkosmos, established in 1985 by the USSR Ministry of General Machine Building, had been actively seeking international partnerships to commercialize Soviet space technology. This collaboration aligned with their objectives of promoting the Soviet space industry in global markets and managing complex international space projects. The USSR's experience with commercial space ventures dated back to the late 1980s when Glavkosmos began offering launch services to compete with US providers.

Our potential partnership with Glavkosmos was particularly timely, as it coincided with a period when the Russian space industry was adapting to the post-Soviet era and seeking new commercial opportunities. The dissolution of the USSR in 1990 had led to significant changes in the space sector, with Glavkosmos transitioning from a Soviet to a Russian entity. For Cancom, this presented a unique chance to leverage Russian space capabilities, which were built on the foundation of Soviet expertise, and potentially expand our satellite services.

It was the 1990s, and Gorbachev's policies of *glasnost* (openness) and *perestroika* (restructuring) had replaced the ubiquitous *nyet* in Russian parlance.

Cancom's CFO and our VP of New Business Ventures made scouting trips to Moscow, accompanied by our Russian military liaison (likely from the GRU, though this wasn't explicitly confirmed), to meet with executives and staff from Glavkosmos and assess the feasibility of the deal. This was during the transitional period following the dissolution of the USSR in 1990, as Glavkosmos was adapting from a Soviet to a Russian entity.

The VP informed me that the Glavkosmos staff had a copy of Cancom's Annual Report and had apparently mocked him behind his back because his boss was a woman. They even waved the page with executive photos and pointed at mine. I found their reaction amusing, though our VP was clearly uncomfortable with the situation.

This incident highlighted the cultural differences and gender biases we were encountering in our international business dealings, particularly with former Soviet institutions that were still adjusting to the new global business landscape.

My trip to Russia was truly the experience of a lifetime. Accompanied by my EVP, Claude, we were fortunate to have an exceptional young interpreter from Georgia, USSR, who spoke five languages, including Mandarin and Japanese, and his native language, Ossetian, despite never having left the Soviet Republic. He was the son of a Georgian party boss, and I often wonder how his life has unfolded since then.

We stayed at the former Warsaw Pact guest house, a sign of changing times. Fortunately, friends had warned us to bring tinned sardines and crackers, as one evening we were shooed away from the guest house dining room by staff saying, "No food. No eat. Go away." Breakfast wasn't much better.

Our interpreter seemed to have universal access to the Kremlin, a privilege that was rare during the Soviet era. After a tour of the Kremlin Armoury Museum, where I admired the Fabergé eggs and was awestruck by the tiny size of Catherine the Great's coronation dress (which indeed had a remarkably small waist), we walked into Red Square.

Coincidentally, we arrived during a break in the 28th and final Congress of the Communist Party of the Soviet Union, which was taking place in July 1990. It felt like a grand spectacle, with a remarkable array of national dress displayed by delegates from the fifteen Soviet republics. Here was the multinational character of the USSR, even as it was on the brink of dissolution. The international press, gathered to cover this historic event, found our presence as Western business visitors distinctly odd and out of place.

After a few days of sporadic meetings, I signed an official agreement with the Soviet officials to work together on our joint satellite venture. We attended a celebratory dinner in what appeared to be an upscale Moscow restaurant, although the meal featured sausages once again, a staple in Soviet cuisine.

Over dinner, I attempted to ascertain crucial planning details, such as the interest rate they proposed for net present value calculations. However, no specific financial information was forthcoming. Instead, we were treated to an unexpected and lengthy medley of Beatles songs performed by the Soviet senior officials, some of whom displayed impressive vocal talents. This musical interlude highlighted the global impact of Western pop culture, even behind the Iron Curtain.

We were also granted the rare privilege of visiting the top-secret Glavkosmos (later Roscosmos) mission control center in the Moscow suburbs. There, we had the opportunity to speak with cosmonauts, both veterans and active duty, offering a unique insight into the Soviet space program.

Back in Canada, I received a copy of a Russian Act of Parliament endorsing our joint initiative. Unfortunately, by 1991, Gorbachev had left office, and all plans for collaboration with Russia were abandoned.

In a similar vein, my EVP and I were later asked by the Canadian government to attend a meeting with representatives of Brazil's satellite agency on behalf of Spar Aerospace, Canada's lead satellite supplier, to foster cooperation and trade. It was a fascinating glimpse of diplomacy at work, although we did not succeed in selling anything. However, I learned that at a diplomatic dinner, where some diners follow different etiquette rules or none at all, it is the diplomat's job to follow custom, and the diplomat's spouse's job to follow the lead of the "differently mannered," ensuring everyone is comfortable.

In April 1992, *The Toronto Star* published an article titled "Why She's at the TOP," which featured a flattering photo of me. The piece was subtitled "High Profile" and included numerous complimentary quotes regarding my performance as CEO, many from individuals who depended on me for their livelihoods. Doug Holtby, who was then the chair of Cancom and CEO of Western International Communications, praised both the company and my leadership, stating, "She's just such a tremendous talent."

I had the opportunity to showcase my expertise in that article as well. I described my "multiple option selection system" to the *Star*'s reporter, a method akin to the one Tom Wolfe detailed in *The Right Stuff*. When confronting a challenging situation, it's crucial to be aware of your range of options and persistently apply them or devise new ones until circumstances determine the outcome. In the context of a test pilot, this process continues until a resolution is reached or, in the most extreme case, impact with the ground occurs.

Thirty years later, I was seated in the front seat of a corporate jet heading north to the oil sands operation at Kearl Lake. The pilot announced that the flaps were malfunctioning, and we would have to return to the jet port an hour away. I could see into the cockpit as the copilot feverishly paged through laminated pages held together with binder rings, stopped, read for a minute, then said something to the pilot. The pilot would twiddle a dial, wait, shake his head, and they'd repeat the process. At one point, we flew at a 45-degree angle for a while. That was a multiple option selection system in action, and we landed safely to a coterie of fire engines. I declined the second attempt at our destination that night. We were going to be too late for dinner anyway.

CHAPTER TWENTY-ONE

Never a Dull Moment

LICENSE RENEWALS, REGULATORY hearings, annual meetings, and new projects all occurred routinely in the life of Cancom, keeping us perpetually busy. William and I had eloped in late 1990 and now had a blended family of five children: William's two grown daughters and my three children.

Fortunately, many years earlier, I had read *Cheaper by the Dozen*, a book about being raised by two pioneering time-and-motion experts, Frank and Lillian Gilbreth. Frank, the father, died of a heart attack in his mid-fifties, and Lillian, a remarkable industrial engineer, inventor, and mother of twelve, continued working into her nineties. When my brother studied at MIT, she was one of his professors. *Cheaper by the Dozen* seemed like a good guidebook to me.

With time, experience, and my father's emphasis on honesty in business and elsewhere, I had come to place a high value on integrity. Thrilled to receive an honorary fellowship from Ryerson University (as the university was then known), I saw a chance to talk about it. I concluded my convocation speech with these remarks:

> I was privileged to sit at the head table at a luncheon organized to laud a businessman who had, unfortunately, passed away before his day of special recognition had arrived. A captain of Canadian industry had been asked to give the address at the luncheon, and 400 or so people

had gathered for the event. The room was appropriately hushed for the presentation, as befitted a eulogy. As the speaker came to conclude what was, overall, a very admiring speech, he paused and said: 'In his life, —— (the deceased) excluded integrity.'

No one laughed; we realized that what we had just heard was an inadvertent error in pronunciation. But what an error!

So that is my message. Live your life so that if someone says in your eulogy, 'In (your) life, you excluded integrity,' everyone present is certain it was an accidental error of pronunciation, not an indictment.

A few busy months later, I was greeted at the office one afternoon by the concerned face of my assistant. "Doug Holtby has been trying to reach you all morning. I explained to him you were at a doctor's appointment, and he asked that you call right away on your return."

Anxiously, I hurried into my office and dialed Doug's office in Vancouver.

"Sheelagh, I am so glad you called. I have been sitting here worrying about you. Are you OK?"

"Well, Doug," I said slowly. "This will be a rather unusual discussion to take place between a president and the chair of the board. I was at the doctor's office to hear the results of my amniocentesis. It looks like in six months or so, William and I will be having a healthy baby."

"A baby! Oh, thank heavens! I was afraid you had cancer."

Then Doug and I launched into a discussion of how we would handle the situation, which, for me, was a tried-and-true approach. I would work, have the baby, and then work some more.

And that is how it went.

I can't take much credit for eliciting such a fantastic comment from Doug. I think what I was learning, through necessity, is that in many instances, if you don't present something as a hurdle to overcome and just take it in stride, it is difficult for someone else to challenge your approach.

As we progressed, Cancom continued to launch innovative and ambitious projects, experiencing both successes and setbacks. In one instance, I overruled my increasingly large belly—disregarding my growing intuition—and later came to regret it. We embarked on a business venture to provide television channels featuring automotive accidents and thrilling moments from motorsports events, such as stock car races and Formula One, to English-style pubs. The aim was to complement the pubs existing entertainment offerings, which included football matches, hockey games, and curling competitions. At the time, this concept appeared promising.

Our potential partners were unfamiliar to us, and Canada was unfamiliar to them. They were using different technology, their research was not very good, but our work team was keen and had a good track record of managing complex undertakings. So, I ignored my qualms, and we made a modest beginning.

The board approved our innovative "car racing highlights" channel, but it turned out my gut was right. Luckily, we weren't too far along, and our CFO was able to minimize the damage, but it was a painful and embarrassing lesson. It really bothered me on behalf of all females when I overheard at least one of the directors insinuating that perhaps my brain had been a bit befuddled by pregnancy. I wanted to bite him on the arm.

But I didn't, and Cancom generally continued to prosper. Some months later, I postponed my departure for work to participate in the final board meeting of Sterling Trust via phone. We had been squeezed by the recession and were now entering into a sale to Laurentian Bank.

I arrived at my office to the news that Allan Taylor, CEO of the Royal Bank, was trying to reach me. I called back and spoke to his secretary. She informed me that he would like to come out (from downtown Toronto to neighboring Mississauga) to meet with me on an important matter and asked if I would be available next Tuesday. Clueless, I said yes, but Tuesday was my due date, and I might not be at work. "Good," she affirmed briskly. "He will be there at 11:30."

And he was. And I was too, resplendent in my navy blue maternity work suit with a purple tie, which William said "set it off perfectly."

I had never met Mr. Taylor, and he didn't bat an eye. Sitting comfortably in my office, he explained to me that the bank board recruitment committee had asked him to invite me to join the Board of Directors of the Royal Bank. He was aware that I had recently resigned as a director from Sterling

Trust and hoped I could join the Royal Bank Board for meetings at my earliest convenience. Startled, I said "Yes."

Nicholas was born a few days later, on March 18, 1993, and not long after, I attended my first meeting of the Royal Bank Board, which was held in New Brunswick's Saint Andrews-by-the-Sea. Nick and his carer came along for the scenery and the food.

Years later, Allan confessed to me that no one had warned him that I was pregnant, much less nine months pregnant, and upon meeting me, he simply decided to carry on, and it all worked out fine.

In the meantime, I felt very honored.

I was not the first woman on the board of the Royal Bank. Sometime in the late 1970s, a large fuss had been made when one of the Canadian bank presidents said there were no women on his board because there were no women qualified for the position. When I joined the Royal Bank Board, there was a woman from Quebec City, a woman from Montreal, and a woman from Western Canada, all of whom seemed very well-qualified.

Today, the Royal Bank of Canada's board has a female Chair, Jacynthe Côté, and women comprise five out of thirteen members. This represents a significant change from the past when bank boards were considerably larger. When I joined, I believe we had thirty-one members, which made it challenging for individuals to make meaningful contributions due to the sheer size of the group.

Not long after joining the Royal Bank board, I was invited by Bob Peterson, the CEO, to join the board of Imperial Oil. Notably, Imperial Oil had included a woman on its board of five independent directors since its inception, and it wasn't long before there were two female directors.

* * *

"And from far and near came the cry of 'Oil!'"

CHAPTER TWENTY-TWO

Walking in the Footprints of Ross Perot

MY MATERNAL GRANDMOTHER, a skilled tailor and needleworker with a penchant for reproaching children, often said, "Idle hands are the devil's plaything." She may have been right, though I'm still working on finding out.

In mid-summer 1993, a friendly Toronto executive recruiter insisted I "must meet" his client, who was seeking a CEO for an information technology firm. I suspected it might be SHL Systemhouse, a reputable Canadian IT company with an impressive market share. Despite my packed schedule, I agreed to an interview, adhering to my "nothing ventured, nothing gained" philosophy.

The interviewer turned out to be a senior vice president from Electronic Data Systems (EDS). At that time, my knowledge of EDS was primarily limited to Ross Perot's multiple U.S. presidential campaigns and his conflicts with the General Motors board, where he famously referred to the directors as "pet rocks." However, Perot had long since departed EDS, having sold the company to GM in 1984. Despite Perot's predictions of failure, his corporate successors continued to run a successful IT outsourcing business, which had expanded globally and diversified its services.

EDS Canada's largest customer was General Motors, and the parent company in Plano, Texas, was looking to diversify and grow.

I found Gary, a plain-spoken Midwesterner from EDS, likable, and I was characteristically forthright with him. Our conversation was relaxed, and, as I prepared to leave, I was surprised by a request to answer a few questions for a videographer set up in the next room. Gary explained that he intended to record various candidates answering a few surprise questions to discuss with his colleagues back in Plano. While most of the questions have faded from my memory, one stands out: he asked what I would bring to EDS if selected for the position.

Scrambling for inspiration and acutely aware of my limited IT knowledge, I smiled into the camera and replied, "I would give EDS Canada a human face." Then I went home to feed the baby.

As an economic nationalist, I had recently realized that every company I'd worked for since my MBA had either "Canada" or "Canadian" in its corporate name. In EDS's case, "Canada" was in brackets at the end.

It was midsummer, and William, Nick (now almost five months old), Matthew, Dan, and I were planning a seaside holiday in Ogunquit, Maine. Our cabin was sparsely furnished with no telephone, and we were all ready for a real rest. Gary called just before we left Toronto, insisting it was vital that I come to Plano immediately to meet the top executives. William volunteered to drive the three boys on the overnight trip via Montreal to Maine. (I later learned that Nick's first night without his mother and her bosom was "challenging.")

I flew to Plano with breast pads and clothing designed to conceal any potential leakage. I arrived in time to share an elegant dinner with Gary and the Executive VP. The following day, I made the rounds, engaging in discussions on various topics, including art, which seemed relevant to the corporate culture. I was told there was one other candidate, the Canadian CEO of an established IT company.

During the interviews, I made a point of emphasizing my lack of IT knowledge. EDS's smiling response to my concerns was, "Sheelagh, we have over 140,000 people who are highly trained and knowledgeable about IT; we have very few who are skilled in strategy."

I bid farewell to Plano with relief, reminding Gary that I was going somewhere without phones but would call him when I returned to Toronto in two weeks.

William swears that Nick propelled himself through the air from his arms to mine across the entire Arrivals floor of Boston's Logan airport. We then settled in for a holiday of lobster and seaside fun.

The next morning, we returned from the sand dunes around 1 pm to find a note taped to our screen door: "Phone Gary in Plano, urgent" with a number.

The nearest public phone was about 10 miles away on the outside wall of Walgreen's in Wells, Maine, beside the empty grocery carts. William waited in an Adirondack chair while I returned Gary's call. Ten mosquito bites later, I returned with the news that EDS wanted to hire me as president and CEO to run their company in Canada, offering a handsome salary and benefits. My response had been, "Could I think about it and call you back?"

The next day, covered in Bug-Off, I called back. William and I had discussed their offer, and he convinced me to test their determination by asking for a 10 percent higher salary. To this day, I rue my answer to Gary's question, "Would that be in Canadian dollars or US?"

Feminism played a role in propelling me toward this new venture. I felt the support of influential women like Simone de Beauvoir, Betty Friedan, Germaine Greer, Robin Morgan, Adrienne Clarkson, and Betty Harragan. Even Xaviera Hollander, the "Happy Hooker," would have given me a fist pump. I was living the life to which I felt entitled.

* * *

On the Right Wavelength

After a stellar career at Cancom, Sheelagh Whittaker takes the president's job at EDS Canada.

* * *

"Heading up part of a multinational firm (EDS is headquartered in Dallas, Texas, and is a wholly owned subsidiary of General Motors) and at the same time being involved with the "'convergence of technology' was an irresistible challenge." . . . "EDS worldwide, offers me a lot of opportunity if I can prove myself in Canada, and that's appealing," says Whittaker, who terms the impending split with Cancom as amicable. . . .

Cancom has a staff of 30 . . . in contrast to EDS Canada's staff of 1600. . . .

"I used to get upset when I read stories in *Chatelaine* about the fast track and the mommy tracker, because I always thought you could have it all . . . but in having it all you have to establish priorities. You don't need to do everything personally." . . .

"At times when I thought I might be doing something controversial, I've made a point of not asking what people thought." . . .

"She has an excellent sense of what is good for her," says Whittaker's sister. "When she makes tough decisions she is prepared to be criticized but she has the strength to know that it's right for her, and go ahead and do it."

The Financial Post Magazine, October 1993, p. 14

On reflection, I just can't resist including another quotation from that article.

Duncan McEvan, former executive producer of CBC's *Venture* and *Life: The Program*, calls Whittaker a 'modern boss' with an 'immaculate mind.'

It's like being the Virgin Mary and Margaret Thatcher all in one.

When Gary saw the article, he advised me to be cautious about it around Plano, since it mentioned I'd had a "sixteen-year relationship with a journalist" that had produced children. Poor Mike.

CHAPTER TWENTY-THREE

November 6, 1993: Who Should Be Nervous?

NICK, NOW A mature seven-month-old, was covering his tray with mashed banana while I tried to keep my work clothes out of his grasping hands and eat a nutritious breakfast in preparation for my first day at EDS.

"How do you feel about starting your new job?" asked Elli, Nick's nanny, as she wiped banana from inside his ear.

"Nervous. I feel nervous," I replied. "Here I am, starting as president of a new company, and I don't know anyone there."

"Ah," said Elli wisely. "You shouldn't be feeling nervous; they should be."

And I guess she was right. I had been hired for my ability to shape and direct a company, and that day marked the beginning of a new direction for EDS Canada.

There were some bumps in the road at first.

When I arrived at the office, my new assistant, Laurie, showed me around.

"This is your office," she said, "and here, next door, would be your conference room."

"*Would* be?" I looked into the room. It was fitted out like an executive's office, complete with award trinkets, a Robert Bateman serigraph, and a lot of business books with uncracked spines.

"Yes, John (my predecessor at EDS) has moved in here until his retirement officially starts. He is available to give you advice if you need it."

Yikes! I thought, remembering how my new boss in Texas, Gary, had characterized his expectations of my presidency. According to Gary, John had done an adequate job yesterday, but it had become clear that he didn't know how to handle today, let alone tomorrow.

"John will be in around 10:30," Laurie added.

"Betty Harragan, where are you and your corporate gamesmanship pointers when I need you?" I implored silently.

So that is how I began at EDS Canada. Sensitive to my lack of IT skills, I received a letter from Gary outlining his expectations for the next year. There was no mention of John. By now, John was ensconced next door, and I began to wander around introducing myself, hoping for a neon arrow to descend from the ceiling showing me the strategic direction in which I should lead the business. In my experience, new directions are best not forced.

Over the next month, I started to get to know members of my team, their strengths and weaknesses, and what they did every day to advance our position in the marketplace. I also found that circumstances had provided a kind of rudimentary political acumen test for my direct reports.

Those who continued to disappear into John's "office" to discuss ideas and initiatives with him, and who had him sign documents and approve expenditures (technically illegal as he no longer had any authority), I put in the "slow on the uptake" category. Those who put their head around my door on the way to John's office to tell me what they were up to, I categorized as "promising." And those who came to meet me with a clear-cut agenda and concrete proposals earned a place in the "Keepers" file.

Poor Laurie had to walk the delicate line between John, who treated her like a daughter, and me, who planned to treat her as a professional assistant and a friend.

After about four weeks of this, Gary flew up to see how I was doing. We were going to review some numbers and talk about plans for the coming year. A few hours into our meeting, Gary said, "Sheelagh, what would you like me to do for you?"

"Get John out of that office," I replied firmly, pointing toward my erstwhile conference room.

"Oh," said Gary, unaccustomed to such a direct call for action.

I thought about comparing myself to Oliver Cromwell having to initiate reforms with a headless Charles I in his state chamber, but I wasn't sure whether seventeenth-century English history featured large in Gary's engineering background.

Instead, I assured Gary that John's active contributions to the future of EDS Canada could now come to a permanent end, and my unfettered regime could start, although I didn't use quite those words.

By day's end, Gary had suggested to John that he could now take his corporate recognition trinkets and go home to begin his well-earned retirement, and I had a conference room.

I don't know if I thought about this then, but I have certainly thought about it since. You have two natural enemies in business leadership: your predecessor and your successor. I can't remember whose maxim that was, but it is ever true! (My friend Pierre at Cancom was a refreshing exception.)

John was my predecessor at EDS Canada, and another John was my successor. Clearly the fates were aware of my strong preference for symmetry at least.

CHAPTER TWENTY-FOUR

Back at the Ranch

FOR MY SECOND visit to EDS HQ in Plano, I was instructed by Corporate to wear cowboy boots and Western clothes. Apparently the global meeting was going to have a Western theme. I bought a nice denim dress and paired it with a red vest and a red cowboy neck scarf.

My equally new colleague, Micael Cimet from EDS Mexico, didn't read the fine print in the advance information. When he arrived at Head Office and saw me decked out in cowboy clothes, he thought, "Wow, this woman has cajónes to dress like that when she comes to Head Office." An hour later, he was over at the Galleria buying cowboy boots for himself.

Micael and I were part of a unique administrative unit called EDS Americas (non-US). I loved the brackets.

Back in Canada, now that I had gained the use of my conference room, I focused on figuring out what we at EDS Canada might accomplish. I had only a vague idea of the shape of the industry we were in or where it might be going, but I could already see that we had a lot of raw capability waiting for direction.

EDS's business in Canada at the time was focused on providing General Motors with IT innovation, expertise, and outsourcing, a related Toronto-Dominion Visa card, and a computer and software reseller business. However, Human Resources Canada had just awarded an EDS-led consortium the contract to bring the administration of the Canada Pension Plan into line with service expectations of the twenty-first century. The

City of Toronto had signed up for some check processing business, and we were working on the Teranet project. So it looked like we were on our way.

I had a great advantage at EDS Canada: I had been personally recruited by the man in Texas to whom I would directly report. It makes a huge difference when you are someone's personal choice. For one thing, he trusted me. And for another, he felt he owed me something because he knew deep down that he had slightly misrepresented what I was getting into.

Those around me gave me a lot of latitude, especially my assistant, Laurie. More than a lot. Laurie covered for me for years, without a word of reproach, until I finally faced up to the challenge of becoming computer literate. Even then, she recently described me this way: "I used to have a boss who didn't like to use her computer, but now she's pretty proficient at it!"

Thirty years later, I learned that Ross Perot, founder of EDS, never used a computer either. Perot was known for his business acumen and sales ability rather than technical expertise. He hired computer experts to handle the technical aspects of the business.

Financial issues were clear enough. It was the market development side of the Canadian business that needed work. Our global accounts were like a rising tide that lifts all boats. In my first year at EDS, we won the Xerox contract, an important and prestigious global account. For me, it brought more employees and revenue and the chance to make a cherished friend for life: Diane.

Diane McGarry was named president of Xerox Canada in 1994, and I called her up right away to invite her to lunch. EDS Corporate was competing for the Xerox account at the time, but that wasn't the only reason I called. I called her because I was so pleased to see another female president appointed in Canada, and I wanted to make her feel welcome. She told me later I was her first caller.

Diane is a great personality. She is petite, rugged, and smart, and you would definitely want her on your team, whatever game you were playing. We were mutually delighted to have a female executive friend, and even more delighted when she became my customer.

It was Diane herself, not the EDS grapevine, who called me to tell me that EDS had won the global Xerox account. She said, "Get on over here,

Whittaker, so we can have a meeting together with the employees who will be affected by the change, and we can tell them what we have planned." So I drove right over, and we met the employees together. It was a great beginning to that business relationship, and for many years, Canada was seen as the best EDS/Xerox success story.

Not long after, when Maureen Kempston-Darkes was announced as president of General Motors Canada, Diane and I phoned her up right away and invited her to join our club. Maureen was a strong and unique addition to our friendship. She is intelligent and practical and a world-class expert in trends in automobiles.

The three of us had periodic "power lunches" in out-of-the-way gourmet restaurants where the three women howling with laughter at the corner table failed to attract any special attention.

I was a bad influence. Maureen and Diane usually wanted to talk about serious issues like inculcating a culture of genuine leadership in the modern corporation or how to provide meaningful employee recognition, at least until the first (large) glass of wine was consumed. For my part, I wanted to talk and laugh about political gossip or new movies. I usually got my way in the end.

The serendipity of our promotions was in part the product of Canada's branch plant economy, which allowed large multinational firms to experiment with appointing women in an environment where not too much global harm could be done to reputation or performance—a bit like test marketing handbags for dogs in Edmonton.

Diane, Maureen, and I shared very little in the way of personal style, but we all had one thing in common: we knew how to do our job. We were part of a dawning moment for women in Canadian business. And while we were working away at our respective businesses, we were joined in the marketplace by other interesting, successful, and fun women, most of whom were branch plant presidents.

Looking over the commentary on women's advancement in the workplace, some themes emerge. For example, the October 20, 1997, edition of *Maclean's* cover declared: "Canada's Top Women CEOs. They have blazed a trail to the top of the corporate heap. But they are few in number and they have paid a heavy price."

Personally, I felt the "heavy price" theme was meant to discourage other women, and it was inaccurate, too. There was no way that the women I knew weren't strong enough to choose another path if they felt too conflicted or burdened. The subtitle of the story inside the magazine was: "To reach the pinnacle of corporate success takes drive, brains, and a sense of humor." Now that's a description I am happy to endorse.

It was October 1999, and I was on the verge of learning how to use a computer when *The New York Times* reported "Cracks in Canada's Glass Ceiling." I must admit I laughed at the photo of myself accompanying the article. I am positioned under a recessed ceiling light in a manner that makes me look like I emit a huge halo, although my true friends have reassured me that it is only a bit exaggerated. The article observes, "In the last decade, as social and economic changes have swept the country, women have suddenly begun appearing at the pinnacles of corporate Canada."

"How does one sit on a pinnacle?" I wondered.

CHAPTER TWENTY-FIVE

A Stranger in a Strange Land

FOR A LONG time, until this very day of writing, I thought I was suffering from imposter syndrome. When I associated with people who attended Ivy League colleges or were descended from agricultural barons, I felt like a misfit. However, I've come to realize that imposter syndrome is characterized by a lack of clear self-perception and anxiety about one's place in the world.

And that's not me. I know who I am, and I understand why I don't always fit in. My starting point was different, and I often see things from a unique perspective compared to those around me.

Robert Heinlein's book *Stranger in a Strange Land*, published in 1961 when I was fourteen (though I believe I read it in 1970), tells the story of a human who comes to Earth as a young adult after being born on Mars and raised by Martians. The novel explores his interaction with our world from the perspective of someone without preconceived notions.

The original "stranger in a strange land" was Moses, and Heinlein's title is a direct quotation from the King James Bible (Exodus 2:22). To be a stranger in a strange land is to feel odd or out of place—a sensation I've often experienced. Male/female, Westerner/Easterner, privileged/not, nuanced/gauche . . . a woman with the occasional lack of *savoir-faire*. While my family and perhaps a couple of early boyfriends or colleagues might object to being cast as Martians in this analogy, some of them could certainly be described as otherworldly.

Analogies aside, Heinlein used his main character's open-mindedness to "challenge social norms" and think afresh about why and how society has decided to do things, and how those conventions might be changed.

This approach of using an outsider's perspective to examine and critique societal norms is not unique to Heinlein. Other authors have employed similar techniques to explore various social issues, particularly those related to gender roles and feminism.

Margaret Atwood has been writing astutely about feminist concerns for most of her career. The first Atwood book I read was *The Edible Woman*, published in 1969. Her later speculative fiction, *The Handmaid's Tale* and *The Testaments*, featuring reversion to historical gender roles and long-standing prejudices, has been broadly recognized as prescient. I'm willing to bet that she often feels like a stranger in a strange land.

Another wise Margaret, the anthropologist Margaret Mead, also played a role in my investigation of life. Her book *Sex and Temperament in Three Primitive Societies*, which I studied in Anthropology 101, was quite an eye-opener for me. Her most salient conclusion is that gender roles are determined by culture, and different societies have very different expectations for masculine and feminine behavior.

Personally, I can relate to this Margaret Mead quotation: "I was wise enough to never grow up, while fooling people into believing I had."

One day in 1985, I happened upon the story of Libby Riddles who was a media sensation because she had just become the first woman to win the famous Alaskan 1,049-mile Iditarod Trail Sled Dog Race. She had struggled through a blizzard to do so.

She was besieged by reporters who wanted to connect her performance to some kind of feminist statement. Instead, she replied with words to this effect: "Isn't what I do testament enough to what I believe?"

CHAPTER TWENTY-SIX

Big Corporations Have Their Own Social Norms

FROM MY TIME on major corporate boards, I vaguely knew that very senior executives in big organizations get to do things far more exotic than having chocolate donuts with sprinkles delivered to the office on Friday mornings. But I wasn't clear on what those things might be.

Then, one morning, several months after I had started working at EDS, I received a memo from head office asking which customers (and their spouses) I was bringing to the World Cup finals at the Rose Bowl in Pasadena.

"I'll show them I'm not in this for the gravy train," I thought piously. "I have lots of work to get done here." So, I wrote back to head office, saying that I was not planning on taking any Canadian customers to that EDS global-sponsored event. Over dinner, I entertained William with the notion of the munificence of it all.

A week or so later, I received an email from head office directed to just a few new global executives, including me, asking us to write a lengthy essay on why we were not taking customers or target customers to the World Cup finals. Well, I'm not *that* slow on the uptake, so that evening over dinner, I announced to William that we were going to visit Los Angeles in July and watch the semi-finals and finals of the World Cup with some other like-minded Canadian couples who were already or might become customers of EDS.

It was a tremendous amount of fun. Our outdoor buffet dinner at the hotel had been arranged with the EDS (non-US) executives and customers at a table of our own. As the evening progressed, my colleague Micael's Latin customers got more and more relaxed, even the Canadians were getting a bit goofy, and the Mexican staff of the hotel started surreptitiously delivering the good champagne to our table.

By the time we joined in with the full-voiced "Ai, yai, yai, yai's," most of the other guests and their hosts had already departed.

The next day, the route for our three EDS buses to the Rose Bowl stadium was blocked at one point, and the passengers on Micael's bus decided to force open the doors and run along the side of the highway for a few miles to ensure they were in their seats on time. The bus I was on was a little late.

Of course, it wasn't all about attending fantastic events, although there were quite a few of them. There was also a significant amount of hard work. When I think about it, I was able to make a major contribution to the company's fortunes by seeing our business with my "fresh eyes." I tried taking executives who were good at federal government sales and contracts out of Ottawa and exposing them to the idiosyncrasies of provincial and local governments or challenging them with our large and complex car industry infrastructure support operations. And our car industry experts were given the opportunity to look at arenas like financial institutions and government.

We set bold goals and mostly achieved them. We had a rock band called the Four Eds, and they played at big company presentations. We helped big business and government unburden themselves of large-scale IT facilities management.

And I sang "Don't Cry for Me, EDS" off-key at a staff results meeting.

Speaking of boards, I was fortunate to be encouraged to maintain my memberships on various boards. In fact, I was specifically asked to accept a position on the Pharmacia & Upjohn Animal Health Board. Those meetings were held in Kalamazoo, Michigan, and it was a whole new world for me. My board colleague, the Dean of Veterinary Medicine from Cornell, and I paid close attention to the idiosyncrasies of the animal health business and jointly admired the amazing original Norman Rockwell paintings arrayed along the hallway in the head office.

I was shocked when the chief operating officer of EDS, Jeff Heller, called to tell me that I had been named an Officer of the parent company, EDS Corporation. Over time, I learned that the honor mainly meant having your name in small print in the annual report and extra scrutiny of your expense reports by the external auditors, but it felt like success. I liked Jeff a lot, and during our conversation, I mentioned to him that I felt especially honored as I realized that my slightly eccentric approach to management, sprinkled with my feminist ideals, had made me unpopular over time with some of those working at head office.

"Oh, Sheelagh," he assured me, "Of course, you have your detractors." And he left it at that.

"You have your detractors" is a phrase to conjure with.

CHAPTER TWENTY-SEVEN

The Times (and the Locations) They Are a-Changin . . .

THE 1990S WERE a period of boom-and-bust for the IT industry. The "e" world was rapidly emerging, and it was hard for big companies to keep pace. In August 1998, the EDS Board decided they needed a different CEO for changing times. Les Alberthal left, and Richard H. Brown (a.k.a. Dick Brown) was hired as head of the parent company.

Dick was known for his aggressive management practices and cost-cutting measures. Before operations in parts of the EDS diaspora (like Canada) even knew it, he was firing people and rearranging the business. In large global businesses, there is a tendency to alternate structures between geographic or horizontally based organizations and vertical product-aligned management. We had been living in the former, and now we were abruptly reorganized into four vertical product lines: outsourcing, business-to-business, e-business, and consulting.

The bulk of the business and revenue was still in outsourcing, which became my main responsibility. However, I also had to find a near-equivalent office in my suite for the new head of e-business, who had just arrived from elsewhere. I was relieved when the new lead for business-to-business assured me he already had perfectly fine accommodations in

Oshawa, Ontario, adjacent to our GM operations. The consulting team was adept at integrating themselves into the organization.

We successfully navigated the widely anticipated Year 2000 (Y2K) computer issues with minimal disruption. Some critics argued that the concerns had been overblown, suggesting we had made a fuss over nothing. However, we firmly believed that without our Herculean preparatory efforts, countless business transactions could have been lost or corrupted due to computer systems failing to properly handle the transition to the year 2000.

Most of my close colleagues in Dallas had either been pushed out by Brown or had chosen to exit. Work became rather confusing and depressing, so much so that one day my assistant caught me crying quietly at my desk. Then, out of the blue, I was asked if I would be willing to take on new leadership responsibilities in the Asia Pacific region, with an emphasis on Australia. "Yes, please. How soon?" was my spontaneous answer.

I was sorry to leave all the colleagues and friends I had made in the Canadian IT industry. As a parting gift, the EDS team won the highly competitive Bank of Canada Retail Bond Processing assignment. My bonus for that win was the acquaintance of a deputy governor of the Bank of Canada, Sheryl Kennedy. She has continued to prosper and has also become a lifelong friend.

More than twenty-five years later, I received an extraordinary appraisal from my then corporate counsel, Richard. Richard was there on my first day to welcome me to EDS Canada. He always had an office strategically located near mine, and he remained a good friend long after I had left for Australia and other parts unknown. These days, we share a pub lunch every few months, and when I told him I was writing this book, he sent me this appraisal.

Leadership and Living

Since you told me you were writing this book, I have been noodling about some of the things about Leadership, and about Living (because these are really life lessons, and they are probably more important), that I learned from working with you. I thought I would share some of the things I learned that have had an influence on my work, my career and my happiness. I haven't tried to gussy these up. They are not profound, these are very colloquial, but they show your impact.

<u>Leadership is not about being involved in every decision</u>. I have taken to heart your admonition not to bring every issue to you. You didn't need to be involved in everything. As I think I have mentioned, you expressed it to me more poetically, "If the issue can't be summarized in a two-page memo, double-spaced, fourteen-point font, it's not at my level."

There is so much encapsulated in this from a leadership perspective. There is hiring the right people. There is trusting the people you have hired. There is empowering them. There is requiring them to do their job, what you are paying them for. There is not feeling threatened by surrounding yourself with hardworking, smart, ambitious people. There is not looking over your shoulder suspiciously at your co-workers. There is preserving yourself for the issues that need your direction, insights, and expertise. There is being a role model for others.

But there is also a personal aspect to this. Take responsibility. Be prepared to accept the consequences of your actions. Apply your expertise. Don't pass the buck. Meet your challenges. Be a grown up.

<u>Business relationships work best when there is some "relationship" in the relationship</u>. You always made sure you had a personal relationship with executives at our clients. This isn't just the story you told me about developing a relationship with a particular client with the hope that if the decision to go with our firm was in the balance, she would say to her team, "Let's go with Sheelagh's team." And it wasn't just because it made life much more enjoyable when you could laugh (which you did) with the people we were doing business with. It's

because our business didn't really work unless there was a relationship with our clients. No matter how long the contracts were that we wrote (and there were a lot of very long ones), it was not possible to cover off every issue, to address every possibility, to lock the client up so tight they could not do something bad. What made for successful business relationships was the white space between the lines. And that was the personal contact between representatives of the two parties that meant that, when there was something to celebrate; it could be a joint celebration and, when there was a problem, there was a problem-solver on the other end to speak with.

With apologies, I referred to this at one point by saying, "We are involved in business marriages, not business one-night stands." They were transactions that lasted for many years. Our business was all about relationships and you made sure there was always some relationship in the relationships.

<u>Remember, and mimic, examples of grace, not examples of getting even</u>. This is a lesson I have carried with me for 25 years. You made a lot of changes when you came to EDS. And they improved many things, including our financial performance and the number of people who wanted to do business with us. One of your executives took credit publicly for your initiatives. I found that personally offensive and, frankly, thought he ought to have been slapped down for it. You did not do so. From all public perspectives, it was water off a duck's back. The results of how you acted were that (i) the people you worked with thought the more of you and the less of him and you garnered our respect for being the better person; (ii) we wanted to work harder because we realized that you were working hard for all of us, not just for public recognition you might receive; (iii) we liked working for—there is no better way to put this—an adult; and (iv) it's not worth sweating the small stuff—life is too short.

<u>Teamwork doesn't just happen</u>. This was driven home in so many ways. There were visioning meetings or days when you brought together large groups of managers and executives to discuss strategy, to develop visions, to solve problems. But, at this distance, the examples

that come to mind relate to the SHL Systemhouse transaction and the steps you took to welcome, into EDS Canada, SHL Systemhouse. This really mattered because this was a transaction that was forced on you by Dallas and Dick Brown but one that you were expected to make work. And you did, by creating one team, not separate teams of EDSers and of Systemhousers (as they called themselves).

You made the decision that the merged company would be called, initially, "EDS Systemhouse." When you made that decision, John, the General Counsel at SHL Systemhouse said that that couldn't possibly be true, that you would never recognize Systemhouse to that extent. But you did it to make the Systemhousers feel like they were part of the team. And when we had the planning meetings after the transaction closed, to try to determine how to unify and operate the joint company, you ensured that there were representatives of Systemhouse at the table, helping to craft the go-forward strategy, so that they realized that this was not something being done "to them" but something we were doing together. That was how you created teams, by inviting people to participate and listening to them when they spoke. You helped create people who were proud to say, "I work for EDS."

<u>You remembered the family</u>. This is a very personal story. I worked for another organization for eight years before joining EDS. My wife never ever liked them. Why? Not the long hours. It was mostly because the Christmas party (it was a "Christmas party") each year was a time for the executives and secretaries to party at a downtown hotel until all hours of the night. There was no recognition of the spouses or of the children. The company demanded tremendous things from the staff which impacted the families but refused to recognize, even in the holiday season, the sacrifices they made.

At EDS, you kept the annual party (which I believe we called a "holiday party") going. And the holiday party recognized the families, including the children. It was the company saying thank you to the families for the efforts of the employees. I can't tell you how far that went in making my family understand who I was working for and feel that they too were a part of it.

<u>Do not be afraid to do the right thing</u>. There are lots of ways of expressing this principle. Sometimes we are reluctant to do the right thing because it is hard or because the consequences are unpleasant. This is what I learned watching how you managed the problem that a big contract became after it looked to be such a wonderful deal. It turned out that we had been misled and, in the process of getting the job done, we were likely going to lose $60 million.

But, when we recognized the problem in 1994, we realized we needed to stop the bleeding. That was absolutely the right thing to do. But the consequences of doing so were going to be very serious for a lot of people. The fact that the consequences were going to be serious, and that it would be very hard, didn't stop you from directing us on the way forward. It was our job to do the right thing, to stop the bleeding.

This was important, because it made the team focus on moving forward and dealing with the consequences, not spending our time hoping the consequences did not occur.

<u>Perfect is the enemy of the good</u>. Since that time, I have referred to this as a "two-step" negotiation when talking with former EDSers. If you recall, it took us two sets of negotiations to solve the problem. We were not able to do it in the first round of negotiations, so we took an interim solution that would allow us to deal with the initial set of issues—it was good enough—and live to fight another day. And when that day came, the other day, then we were able to fix things. I learned from how you handled that, "To be practical, not perfect." Had we insisted on solving it completely the first time, we would never have gotten there. But, because we were willing to accept a partial solution, one that let us live to fight another day, we were able to do exactly that, fight on another day.

These are some of the lessons I learned that I carry with me, and for which I thank you.

Best,
Richard

Somewhat surprisingly, EDS globally had highly competent and insightful lawyers with great people skills. Richard is, of course, a friend for life and he always tried to save me when I did stupid things.

CHAPTER TWENTY-EIGHT

Horizontal Emigration

WE PACKED UP and left for Australia quite quickly. The family was adaptable. Abigail and Emily had long since graduated and were busy working, while Meghan and Matthew were still attending university. Daniel, in his final years of high school, found the decision to move difficult. Ultimately, he decided to stay in Toronto because aligning curriculums and school years so close to graduation was too challenging. Matthew, with the help of his father Mike, watched over Daniel and ensured he became eligible for university.

Nick didn't have a choice in the matter, and William, an Australian by birth, embraced the move wholeheartedly.

EDS's two biggest Asia-Pacific customers—the Australian Tax Authority and the Australian Customs and Immigration—were in Canberra, where we settled to begin our new life. The work was challenging. Meeting the IT needs of complex government agencies required a lot of quick thinking and flexibility. Nick attended school in a uniform of a khaki shirt and shorts, complete with a broad-brimmed hat tacked up on one side. William relished his roots, and Carly, our then nanny, moved with us to help keep us on an even keel.

One hallmark of my career was a willingness to hire and properly compensate help, both at work and at home. Having grown up with a live-in housekeeper from a very young age, I understood the importance of domestic assistance and the necessity of treating all types of help fairly.

I passed this practice on to my children, and currently Meghan and I share a housekeeper who has been with one or both of us for over twenty years. I suspect I had the only household in graduate school that intermittently employed a cleaning lady.

The difference in time zones (Canberra is +14 hours ahead of Toronto) meant that I routinely attended "pajama meetings" with the rest of the EDS world. Fortunately, such meetings were audio-only back then. Imperial Oil wired up their boardroom in Toronto, and my board colleagues told me that my occasional interjections during meetings seemed to descend from the ceiling as if from on high. I had been asked by the owners of CanWest Global to be their representative on the board of Network Ten, a Sydney-based TV and advertising operation, in part to help manage the time discrepancy, which provided me with a wonderful perspective on Aussie business.

The business community was welcoming, and we had many relatives in the country.

It turns out that "Sheila," and its Irish variants like Sheelagh, Sheela, and Sheelar, are all long-standing Australian slang terms for a woman or girl. As you might imagine, "Let's go to the pub and get ourselves some Sheilas" is a rough approximation of the regular use of the term. William had never mentioned this to me, but when pushed by others, he answered with pride, "All the men in Australia want a Sheelagh, and I have one."

The 2001 symposium of the International Institute of Communications (IIC) was sponsored by EDS and located in Adelaide, home of another of our major clients, the Government of South Australia. I had been a member of the IIC since my Cancom days and was looking forward to visiting my clients and old friends and to attending the conference.

On the first evening, my conference schedule directed me to attend a dinner to meet officials and politicians from South Australia and a former president of the United States. As I walked into the dining room, I noticed a couple of things immediately: only a few places had been set, and to my immediate right there was a small photography stage with a circular reflector, much like one seen at high school proms. Directed toward the camera setup, I noticed Bill Clinton standing, waiting to have his photograph taken, in this instance, with me.

Caught off guard, I struggled to give him some context in which to place me. EDS executive? Corporate sponsor? South Australian supplier? Then I had it!

"Hello, President Clinton," I said. "I am Sheelagh Whittaker from Canada."

His face lit up with an enormous smile, and he grasped my hands tightly.

"So terrific to meet you," he effused. (Americans don't know about the Aussie understanding of "Sheilas.") It was only a little later that I realized I had been wearing a navy-blue dress very similar to the famous one worn by Monica Lewinsky.

When the official photographs of my encounter with Bill arrived, I sent copies to my children entitled, "Monica Lewinsky in Her Later Years."

Most of my kids found the photo pretty funny. One of the newer members of the extended family, unsure of the extent of my savoir-faire, did ask a family member if I knew who Bill Clinton was.

Later, I realized that day, Tuesday, August 4, 2001, was Census Day in Australia, and that Bill Clinton and I have been memorialized in official Australian Census Records as staying at the same hotel on that day. Top that, Monica!

Joking aside, I have tremendous sympathy for the fact that masculine peccadillos and political self-righteousness came close to ruining Monica Lewinsky's life. In a first-person piece in the July/August 2024 edition of *Vanity Fair* entitled "In Praise of Alternate Endings," she counsels the reader to "Never lose hope."

Despite Germaine Greer's sometimes scathing commentary, improvements in the workplace status of women in Australia were only just gathering momentum during my time there. I encountered numerous outstanding women whose rank or recognition in the marketplace fell short of their deserved status.

Upon reflection, Australia's geographic position has resulted in a more domestically focused economy as compared to Canada. With companies primarily managed by local executives, the opportunity to use subsidiaries or branch plants as "sheltered workshops for women" was more limited. As a result, Australian counterparts to my Canadian friends, like Diane

Monica Lewinsky in Her Later Years

McGarry and Maureen Kempson-Darkes, had to wait longer for significant changes.

Australia and New Zealand take pride in their egalitarian cultures, often undercutting those who try to stand out from the crowd—a phenomenon known as the "tall poppy syndrome." I was fortunate in that I wasn't easily categorized. After all, who has ever heard of a Tall Poppy Sheila? This unique position afforded me more freedom as an outsider to build bridges with customers, speak publicly about the benefits of empowering people to challenge old ways, and acknowledge that even experts can sometimes be wrong.

Our family settled in so well that we purchased a beach unit over the mountains near a golf clubhouse. There we enjoyed fresh fish and chips, and one could play the "pokies" (gambling machines) between the main course and dessert. The establishment even provided a room full of games for children and the supervisor let Nick run it with her.

Just as I was beginning to think of Australia as my "happily ever after place," I was urgently asked to relocate to London to manage some delicate market issues. This move seemed less like a "where should we put her" decision and more of a "this is where we really need her" situation.

William, a longtime Anglophile, greeted the news cheerfully, and Nick knew and liked England from previous visits when his father worked there. Nevertheless, I still feel a little bit guilty about how frequently and abruptly we moved him. We relocated once again.

Years later, when I asked Nick to write about what he had learned during his peripatetic upbringing, he wrote this:

The Millennial—Raised by Feminist Parents or Wolves (depending on who you ask)

By Nicholas Whittaker Morgan

Things my mother taught me:

1. **Budget:** Before I set off to university in Ireland, my mother and I agreed on a spending budget for my first term. Many an hour was spent painstakingly reviewing Irish grocery store prices and restaurants online to try to get a sense of how much my meals would cost. I also learnt it was important to pad the budget where possible and find opportunities to save. Saving on lunch by having a "pot noodle" meant an extra beer or two in the evening. When you have a known and finite source of income (as you do when you're an adult), you spend more carefully.
2. **Invest in Gratitude:** With a large family spread across Australia, the USA, and Canada, I frequently sought lodging at the homes of family and friends while on holiday. Given I was so often a guest in others' homes, my mother taught me the importance of making positive investments in gratitude. I learned that I was much more welcome on a second stay if I had written a thoughtful thank-you note or purchased a gift for my hosts.

3. **Opportunity Cost:** My mother taught me that "opportunity cost" is the value of the forgone alternative when making a decision. It represents the potential benefits you miss out on when choosing one alternative over another. It's not just about the money spent, but also about what you could have gained by choosing a different option.
4. **Avoid Empty Threats:** Mum told me never to threaten something you are not willing to do. Standing your ground and being willing to make a threat in a personal or professional environment is important, but if your threat is empty, you undermine your own credibility and integrity.
5. **Salary Negotiations:** Mum taught me to put more emphasis on winning increases to my base salary than my end-of-year bonus. Bonuses come and go on an annual basis, but through the effect of compounding you can feel the benefits of a salary increase for your whole working life.
6. Lastly, in honor of one of my Mum's best friends, Baroness Margaret McDonagh (tragically deceased), who scolded me on my first professional day of work in the constituency office. She said firmly, "Don't ever show up to a meeting without a notepad and pen." While we live in an increasingly digital world, I've never shown up to a meeting empty-handed again.

*　*　*

Margaret lives on in our hearts.—Mum

CHAPTER TWENTY-NINE

"A Female Leader? And a Colonial at That?"

BEFORE I HAD even learned my new London postal code, the managing director for EDS Europe, a smart and likable guy named Bill, instructed, "See that pile of private-sector focused business over there? Go fix it."

I actually love that kind of under-specified challenge, so I set out to do what he had implicitly asked—make the business profitable and make the customers and the employees happy.

Years earlier, at Canada Consulting, one of my partners had looked at a trenchant Whittaker curriculum vitae prepared for a client proposal and said, "There's a 'need for achievement' resume if ever I saw one." And he was right. Why else would I be writing this book?

History-loving immigrants like me experience the UK environment as a posh Disneyland for adults. I lived near the cluster of embassies on Grosvenor Square and walked to work through Berkeley Square, immersing myself daily in London's rich history. By this point, I felt I had finally acquired enough strategic insight about EDS's operations to be genuinely helpful to both co-workers and customers. My unique distinguishing credential was that, over the years, I had assimilated invaluable expertise from the top down, giving me a comprehensive understanding of the company.

Oyster, our pioneering UK smart card payment system for Transport for London commuters, was among the first and largest of its kind worldwide. Our collaborations with financial institutions and a major brewer were both challenging and rewarding. Navigating the exit from a contract lost to new competitors required a delicate balance of professionalism and grace. It was particularly encouraging to find that the South African government's requirement to appoint black women to senior positions in our SA operations was enthusiastically embraced by our local executives and sales team.

I was able to hire a likeable right-hand person named Sam, who was recommended to me by Ross Perot. Sam was smart and experienced and full of new ideas—a perfect fit, and I am still thrilled that Ross phoned me personally to recommend him. The call would have seemed suspicious except that Ross had a distinct voice that would be very hard to impersonate, and I already knew he and Sam had worked well together at Perot Systems.

My time at EDS UK was like a game of two halves. After eighteen months or so, while attending an office Christmas dinner, Bill stopped behind my chair and said, "Do you fancy taking over the public sector?"

Although slightly inebriated, I knew what he meant and smiled, saying, "Yes."

Bill replied, "That settles it then," and went on his way.

When I got home that evening, I said to William, "I think I am taking over the public sector business, and I am really excited."

"Good on you," he commented, like the Australian he was.

I made only one stipulation. I told Bill that such a job required several years to execute well and that I needed assurance I would be in the job long enough to complete much of what needed to be done. He heartily agreed.

Six months later, he prepared mid-term performance reviews for his direct reports, which included executives covering the UK, Ireland, Africa, the Middle East, and Europe. He told me his rating system involved deciding, if he were in a sinking boat, who he would throw out first. With a smile, he told me that, based on his analysis, I would be the last person he would throw out of the boat. That assessment put a skip in my step.

Sam was promoted to lead the private sector business, which continued to improve steadily. As close colleagues, we shared many experiences, and one day, under the influence of alcohol, he confessed that he admired my style so much that he described me to others as "a woman who clanged when she walked." While not as eloquent as Richard's comments, I appreciated the sentiment nonetheless.

Things were not running as smoothly in Texas, however. Despite the shake-up and cost-cutting, corporate morale was poor, and overall results were underwhelming. After a brief tenure, Dick Brown had been replaced, and Michael Jordan, formerly of CBS and much earlier of McKinsey, became CEO.

Time zones were a still a natural hindrance, and I kept my head down, solving immediate problems and generally ignoring the politics of EDS HQ in Texas.

CHAPTER THIRTY

It Turns Out You *Can* Break a Glass Ceiling Feet First

THE YEAR 2004 presented significant challenges, with our activities ranging from negotiating fair compensation for the cancellation of a major project to preparing a comprehensive reference document for a parliamentary committee on the complexities of managing large-scale IT projects. Additionally, I had the opportunity to testify before parliament, where I shared EDS's insights and expertise.

We also deepened our relationships with UK Justice, Defense, and the Department of Works and Pensions, and won an award for an electronic exhibit-managing process to be used by the courts. The performance of Sam's group was also stellar.

An official performance review was scheduled for me by Bill on November 1st. Other priorities cut the interview to a quick conversation, but Bill did take the time to tell me that, overall, I had an A+ in external business relationships and an A– in managing my political relationship with Plano, Texas. I was pleased with such a positive appraisal. "Works and plays well with others" had never been my forte.

Bill said that we would have a relaxed dinner to discuss my appraisal further and promised to give me advice on how to ensure that people in

Plano better understood how well my actions in business aligned with their own agendas. At Bill's request, the dinner was scheduled first for December, then January, and finally for February 7, 2005. And yet, it never took place because that was the day I was terminated.

Late November 2004 presented a severe crisis. A software upgrade error froze thousands of Department for Work and Pensions computers, threatening to disrupt payments to UK pensioners. Despite the delivery side of EDS being a separate vertical, the responsibility for managing this crisis fell to me as the most senior executive in the country at the time. The gravity of the situation hit home as I listened to the BBC broadcasting our perceived failure while en route to Parliament for an urgent meeting with senior civil servants.

Managing such a complex situation was stressful and demanding, especially with all the US staff away on Thanksgiving holiday. Initially, the problem looked enormous and intractable. But we found ways to solve it quickly and provided the customer with a root cause analysis pointing to our own operator error, which showed we were honest as well as professional.

During this period, my team was developing the concept of "Agile Government," building upon EDS's strategic vision of an agile enterprise. Just days before Christmas, I accompanied CEO Mike Jordan on a tour of key British customers, which was well-received. As we concluded the trip, Mike complimented me on my adept handling of numerous sensitive issues. I believe Michael, with his McKinsey & Company background, had always appreciated my approach to management and problem-solving.

January went well, but the atmosphere among the European executives seemed tense. The 2005 budgets had not been discussed, and there were rumors of a secret report blaming the old boys' network for delivery problems and weakened morale. There was also talk of midnight calls.

Despite that, I attended the annual sales meeting in Dallas in January, feeling that our prospects for 2005 were excellent. In early 2004, the task had seemed truly daunting, but the team had risen to every challenge. Now we had been given very tough targets with the admonition that the Corporation needed our help to free up funds to invest in the future, and we were up for it.

In fact, when Bill called me into his office on the morning of February 7, I was looking forward to telling him about all that we had accomplished lately and that we had signed up to do our share of the impossible. We had concrete plans and the will to carry them through. In addition, I had been advised that confirmation would be coming through within hours that we were among the finalists for the Met Police pursuit. I thought he'd enjoy hearing all the good news and that I'd enjoy delivering it.

But I never got the chance. Instead, I fell through the glass ceiling and landed in Berkeley Square. Luckily, I was wearing low heels.

CHAPTER THIRTY-ONE

"I Ain't Down Yet"

THOSE FAMILIAR WITH me know my penchant for quoting poetry or humming show tune lyrics, sometimes aptly, sometimes not. A serious-minded psychologist might observe this behavior, sigh, and label it as "Typical self-soothing." Whatever it may be, it's a coping mechanism that has served me well.

Throughout my long and largely successful career, I've encountered a wide range of experiences, not all of them positive. Generally, I've been adept at identifying the root of a problem. In response, my subconscious often supplies an apropos lyric or verse. For instance, when faced with a particularly challenging situation, I might find myself mentally singing, "It's my party and I'll cry if I want to, cry if I want to, cry if I want to. You would cry too if it happened to you." Or "I ain't down yet."

Gender has undoubtedly played a role in both my disappointments and my successes. When asked about this on panels or by reporters, I've developed the habit of saying that the early negative impacts of sexism in my career have long since been offset by instances of positive discrimination. I truly believe that the disadvantage of being underestimated as a female has been thoroughly counterbalanced for me personally by opportunities I've received because someone was looking for "a woman on this board," "in this job," or "for this profile."

Once, while serving on the Imperial Oil Board, colleague Krys Hoeg and I attended an employee gathering arranged by HR to give female employees (though males were welcome too) a chance to meet and talk with us. Toward the end of our formal question period, a woman in the audience asked, "What do *you* do when you find yourself in a position where everything seems to have gone terribly wrong, and you just don't know what to do?"

After a long pause, I replied, "Well . . . I drink."

"Me too," said Krys. (I suspect Krys especially liked my answer since she had previously been CEO of a liquor company.)

Everyone laughed. Of course, it isn't always that simple. We all need coping mechanisms to navigate life's inevitable demoralizing, sometimes surprising or shocking, ups and downs.

When stricken, I prefer to go to bed in a cold room under a big eiderdown, hoping that either things will improve or that I'll turn into Rip Van Winkle. Sleep is always a big help for me. Having someone special to talk to is also crucial. William certainly filled that role well.

Once, one of my kids asked what I had learned from being fired. "Not much," I replied.

While waiting for my departure circumstances to become clear, I was invited to various interviews with former competitors, start-ups, and international government agencies. I provided advice to venture capitalists and watched from a distance as both friends and enemies fell from their heights in turn.

Standard Life plc made a determined effort to recruit me as a board member, and I felt very cosmopolitan joining the group in Edinburgh. Back in Canada, I accepted responsibility as a board member for a new type of company called CanWest MediaWorks Income Fund.

What encouraged me most during this time was joining the inaugural VIP Board of the European Professional Women's Network (EPWN). Those accomplished women from across Europe gave me real hope for the future. I still dine out on the fact that Christine Lagarde held one of our first dinner meetings in her apartment overlooking the Eiffel Tower. Shortly thereafter, she was appointed President of the European Central Bank.

I made wonderful new friends during this period. Baroness Margaret McDonagh was a real ally on the Standard Life board, and she frequently asked me to speak to candidates attending courses at her company which offered an executive board training ground for UK-based female executives. They were great courses, with content ranging from tips from a former BBC host on how to present yourself on television to how to support other women in the boardroom. I tried to be practical and encouraging in my presentations to the attendees.

In one instance, Margaret invited me to join her at a workshop with some new board trainees and stay on to listen to the luncheon speaker. Fortunately, we were sitting side by side during the luncheon so I could write a message to her on my paper napkin while no one was watching. I wrote:

"This speaker," (the highly credentialed chair of a really important insurance company) "is really dreadful. She is boring and not very smart."

"Ah, Sheelagh," whispered Margaret. "That's the point. Her speech is a subtle demonstration to the attendees that you don't have to be that smart or even very interesting to achieve high position, sometimes you just need to be in the right place at the right time."

Margaret and I lacked sufficient British Airways travel status to access the BA Lounge at Edinburgh Airport when attending Standard Life Board meetings. We found it embarrassing to see our male board colleagues enjoying complimentary refreshments in the glass-walled lounge while we resorted to Pret A Manger. We voiced our concerns to the Standard Life Corporate Secretary, and subsequently, we were granted honorary BA status.

This experience reinforced our shared belief that no barrier, glass or otherwise, was too formidable for us to challenge and overcome.

CHAPTER THIRTY-TWO

Evolution Makes Up 89% of the Word "Revolution"

AT THIS POINT, you might be wondering what happened to the "I am Woman, hear me roar" theme in my story. However, I took Adrienne Clarkson's advice to heart: "Be a witness to the life to which you feel entitled." I also resonated with Prime Minister Pierre Elliott Trudeau's bold declaration, "Just watch me." These philosophies shaped my approach to both my career and life.

Meanwhile, I walked around my home singing, "I have confidence in confidence alone; besides which, you see, I have confidence in me," a line from *The Sound of Music*. I recently discovered a humorous take on this title by a band called Sludge, which released a record titled "The Sound of Mucus."

And sometimes I write poetry to try to turn feelings into art.

Another Kick in the Stomach

By Sheelagh Whittaker

The corporate adieu
Left me terribly blue
And without much to do
For a grim week or two.
Then I started to look
And came up with a book
About murder (to write)
A fine end to my plight.
Hence thinking and writing
And working and playing
With old friends and new
I've had plenty to do. Whew!

CHAPTER THIRTY-THREE

Varying My Shots

UNBEKNOWNST TO HER, Penny inadvertently set the stage for my "rising phoenix" opportunity. On September 11, 2001, at around 9 PM Canberra time, she called me from Wellington, New Zealand, excited about an amazing story she had discovered on the Internet. Being in the antipodes, neither of us had any inkling that in just a few hours, a plane would deliberately crash into the World Trade Centre in New York, forever changing the course of history.

She explained excitedly that she had found the website of a tiny town in Lancashire where someone had posted newspaper coverage of a murder trial in 1885 involving two women. Her amazement stemmed from the fact that the accused appeared to be our grandmother's stepmother, Grace, and Grace's sister, Isabella. The victim was Grace's two-year-old toddler, Tom, and our grandmother, Margaret Isherwood, aged ten, was a Crown witness. This was the first we had ever heard of this event, and we had known our grandmother well until she passed away, still lucid, in her late eighties. In fact, I am named after her.

A few hours later, I called Penny back in Wellington to wake her up. "Over in New York, where it's still yesterday," I told her, "something horrific and unbelievable is happening."

As the world gradually settled into a new normal following the 9/11 terror attacks, I found myself recalling that Victorian-era newspaper story Penny had mentioned. I thought, "There's a story I might be able to write.

I can start researching on the web and plan a special trip to the Forest of Bowland, the scene of the crime, during my next visit to Britain."

I love reading, especially mysteries, but I have never had the kind of imagination that could conjure up that genre of book. I fall more into the category of knowing how to write a good consulting proposal. But here was a ready-made historical drama where I actually knew one of the players. Surely, I could make something of that.

When I was unexpectedly transferred to Britain by EDS to "fix things" several months later, the family was able to begin taking holiday excursions to the home of my father's forebears, searching through old churches and records for more details of that murder case.

Liberated from the time-consuming demands of my EDS executive role, I suddenly found myself with the luxury of pursuing other interests. My emerging agenda quickly filled with diverse activities, including conducting focused research on the tiny village of Slaidburn in Lancashire, outlining a book, attending board meetings, delivering speeches and presentations, and encouraging women to be "bloody, bold, and resolute" at gatherings of the European Professional Women's Network. Additionally, I enjoyed playing bridge with groups of varying expertise, both mine and theirs. This new chapter of my professional life was rapidly taking shape, offering a rich tapestry of intellectual and social engagements.

Meanwhile, Abigail, Emily, Meghan, Matthew, and Daniel were all experiencing the ups and downs of early adulthood. William and I now had some very adorable grandchildren. Meghan and her spouse spent some time considering living and working in the Caribbean, and, inspired by their house hunt, we bought a beach condo to keep them company. It turned out that they didn't take the job offered there, but we all embraced spending time together by the sparkling turquoise sea whenever possible.

Nicholas, our youngest, having endured more parenting than his siblings, was off at Trinity College in Dublin, learning new things.

CHAPTER THIRTY-FOUR

I Rise Again

We rise again in the faces of our children
We rise again in the voices of our song
We rise again in the waves out on the ocean
And then we rise again.
—The Rankin Family

I QUICKLY DISCOVERED THAT the painstaking process of uncovering historical information about a possible murder, and the likely reason why my Whittaker grandparents emigrated to the wilds of British Columbia at the turn of the twentieth century, was a task right up my alley. Never before had I had the time to steadily pursue such a fascinating subject.

Writing a book about a complex legal case, especially one involving family, demands intense focus and energy, and it's a time-consuming process. Throughout this journey, I gained valuable insights and encountered numerous kind and helpful individuals. Notably, I met Catherine and David Higham, the couple responsible for initially posting the newspaper clipping about the crime on the Web. Their contribution was instrumental in sparking my interest and research.

Catherine and David were locals, and they knew a lot about historical attitudes and habits, most of which had not changed much since 1885. Their sleuthing abilities were extraordinary. Our shared research was initially exchanged by email, and it was a real delight to go up to Slaidburn to meet them and tour the scene of the crime enlightened by their knowledge of the countryside.

Embracing my "bright but undisciplined persona," I approached the writing process without a set timetable. Before I knew it, I had a finished product. William, my beloved husband and former editor of *The Brandon Sun* in the 1970s, edited the manuscript. Despite our lack of connections in the British publishing industry, I remained motivated by the mantra "If you want to, man, you can." Ultimately, it was more serendipity than my spirited initiatives and cold calls that led me to find a Canadian publisher, Dundurn, who expressed interest in my book.

Perhaps best expressed in an essay by my son Matthew Van Dusen in a *Forbes* article, published August 16, 2012, not long after the publication of my book, *The Slaidburn Angel*, and entitled: *"My Mother, Corporate Executive and Family Murder Investigator"*—he wrote as follows: "Retirement from the C-suite, the ad campaigns tell us, should be a senior's wonderland of whale watching, mountain trail hiking, and model ship building, alongside preternaturally patient grandchildren. Sprinkle in a few corporate directorships and perhaps charity work on top, and the years might seem golden indeed.

Also, unspeakably boring.

My dear retired mother, M. Sheelagh Whittaker, was once featured on the front of *The New York Times*' business section as having broken the glass ceiling. She still serves on the boards of British insurance giant Standard Life and Canada's Imperial Oil, which is majority-owned by Exxon. But her main pursuit in retirement has been something altogether more thrilling: a true-life murder mystery in her family's past . . .

In a prologue to the book, she notes that "the trappings of education, job and even friends are ephemeral . . . the only people you can reliably count on are your beloved family." As it turns out, *The Slaidburn Angel* may have been a way for my mother to engage in that most shopworn of retirement goals: spending more time with her family."

Pleased by the overall experience, I wrote another book—a semi-autobiographical novel titled *Evaline: A Feminist's Tale*—which presented a unique set of challenges and advantages. Unlike my previous book, the research for this book was primarily introspective rather than requiring on-site investigation. In the spring 2017 issue of *Women of Influence Magazine*, I was quoted at length about what motivated me to write the book and its meaning.

"One of my main reasons for writing the book," I said, "was to challenge the feminist label, to say to readers, 'This is a feminist—a daughter, and a lover, and a mother, and a laugher and a clever business-person, and a screw-up, and a big success, and someone who is lonely and suffers self-doubt. I wanted to make other women proud to say: 'Yes, I am a feminist.' Or at least to shift their notion of a feminist from a strident ideologue or Justin Trudeau to someone who simply believes in natural justice."

The article continued thus: "Refreshingly, these incidents aren't accompanied by the typical motherly guilt. She recalls her daughter, Meghan, telling a reporter that her mom was always there for her. 'She totally lied,' Sheelagh says with a laugh. 'One of the things I was trying to counter is that an awful lot of young women that I spoke to over time felt guilt. I want to show those women that you can be at peace with the person you are.'"

* * *

Some years later, journalist Harvey Schachter, a man to whom I had written over the years for publishing advice and who had actually provided some, agreed to write a book with me. It was a spontaneous decision sparked by an email exchange. We had never met, spoken, or texted (and still haven't), and we didn't initially plan to constrain ourselves to emails. However, when we realized that this had been our exclusive mode of communication, we decided to continue that way.

The result—*When Harvey Didn't Meet Sheelagh: Emails on Leadership*—is a blend of Helen Hanff's book *84, Charing Cross Road* and insights drawn from Harvey's career as a broadly read business columnist and Sheelagh's experience as a successful female CEO.

The book is full of agreements, disagreements, and insights on leadership, management, and the hurly-burly of the workplace, or lack of same. And it includes a literary scoop.

Harvey and I are patiently waiting for a reason to meet and shake hands, but time is passing.

CHAPTER THIRTY-FIVE

And So It Goes, and So It Goes . . .

THE DESOLATING DEATHS of my much-loved son Daniel and my beloved husband, William, a book or a poem or two, occasional speeches, heart-warming accolades, executive board challenges large and small, a talented mix of grandchildren and a cruise on a marvelous ship filled with successful authors of all sorts, led to my journey to my Caribbean refuge to enjoy Christmas with my family. But an increasingly persistent and debilitating pain in my back was worrying me.

Early morning on December 24, 2021, my son Nicholas and I found ourselves in a neurologist's office, listening to an explanation of an arcane condition called *cauda equina* syndrome. The neurologist's message was clear: I required immediate back surgery. While he called the neurosurgeon away from his Christmas Eve golf game, Nick and I sat in the waiting area, frantically searching our phones for information about the condition. The various online medical sources we consulted unanimously agreed with the neurologist's assessment. Shortly thereafter, when the neurosurgeon arrived, he concurred with the urgent need for surgery.

That evening, I had surgery and was instructed to remain horizontal for at least six weeks.

A team of caregivers was assembled to support me, consisting of my children, who were also juggling their own careers, and some local professional carers. Among these dedicated individuals was Trudy-Ann, a lively Jamaican woman whom the reader may recall from the early pages of this book. Trudy-Ann quickly became one of my most stalwart carers.

In so many ways, as I've noted earlier, Trudy Ann prompted this whole new book. So I called her and asked for her take on our time together, and this is what she wrote:

> My name is Trudy-Ann Ashley. I grew up in a big family with four sisters and five brothers. My dad was around but wasn't very present; alcohol consumed most, if not all, of his salary. My mother was always away working but was more present through letters and phone calls. I was born in Jamaica and grew up there. I started working in Cayman at the age of 21 and have been coming here since I was eight years old. My mom always held at least three jobs here in Cayman. Maybe that's where I got my work ethic from. My mom was always the breadwinner.
>
> When I first met Sheelagh, I heard her laughing as she called out for me to come in. Despite meeting her during a difficult time in her life, you could never tell she was struggling. Sheelagh laughed throughout her pain. I helped her pick out the prettiest dress and apply lipstick, all while she was in discomfort, but we kept laughing as we got it done.
>
> I encouraged her because her life sounded fascinating, and I appreciated that she wasn't afraid to share both the good and bad aspects—because that's what life is about. We all have our ups and downs. Sheelagh is always laughing, even when she's in pain. Her laughter seems to be a constant, regardless of her circumstances.

Thank you Trudy-Ann. You were there when I needed you.—Sheelagh

It has taken some time, and a little prodding by my friend (and publisher) Neil Seeman, who has a lot of experience with women as achievers, but he and Trudy Ann, between the two of them, have to hold themselves responsible for this book. And author and publisher Ken Whyte would have received credit for reminding me that authors like me have to write for love because we sure as hell don't write for fame and fortune, but I already knew that.

CHAPTER THIRTY-SIX

Important Lesson for Me: Second-Wave Feminism Has Had Its Day

ON A RECENT trip to Charleston, South Carolina, I was fascinated by the meticulous efforts made over time to preserve the Confederate character of the city, providing an accurate record of how people likely lived and thought. The bombardment of Fort Sumter marked the start of hostilities in the American Civil War, and tremendous efforts have been made to retain the character of the South through subsequent wars, turmoil, earthquakes, and hurricanes.

During a tour of an antebellum mansion, I learned that we no longer say "slaves" or "slavery"; we say "enslaved." Meghan was surprised that I didn't already know this, but she knows I tend to be a little behind on social changes and likely to commit some terrible faux pas in public. She cringes when I thoughtlessly suggest we proceed in "Indian file." But, as she would say, I am trying.

The word "enslaved" made me think. The days of broadcasters having a correct usage list for words like "chairperson," or my persistent irritation at the use of "manpower" or even "man days," are passing or have passed.

Women have made real progress in the workplace, and we're on to new battles, like LGBTQ+ acceptance and a more disciplined use of words like "autism" to describe a different way of thinking.

I'm embarrassed that I make mistakes and miss nuances, and I struggle with outdated prejudices. I try to imagine how I would have behaved if I had been raised as a Southern Belle or steeped in propaganda concerning the ethics of eugenics. Despite some indications to the contrary, I tend to be a rule follower and hate the thought that I probably would have gone along with the prevailing ignorance.

But it is not too late to educate myself out of prejudice. I was delighted to read *A Brief History of Everyone Who Ever Lived: The Human Story Retold Through Our Genes* by Adam Rutherford. Among other things, in Chapter 5, Rutherford states:

> I am unaware of any group of people on Earth that can be defined by their DNA in a scientifically satisfying way. There are plenty of genetic differences and physical differences that emerge from those genes between people and peoples, but none that align with the way we talk about 'race.'

If I hadn't already begun to think about the life cycle of social movements, like the Second Wave of Feminism, it was brought home to me when I asked my granddaughter Ava, Matthew's daughter, to write something for my book. It serves as my epilogue, for it is the future and the present and the past of feminism: one that reminds us that we owe a lot to those who have come before, betwixt, and after. I am tremendously grateful to have seen what I saw, and I marvel at what's coming next.

A Generation Zee's (Zed to me, but she lives in New York) Take on Feminism

By Ava Quinn Van Dusen, High School Sophomore

My own womanhood is something that I consider often, especially considering I am still somewhat of a girl. There are good and bad parts of that. Reflecting on feminism, though, the experiences of my grandmother differ from mine in half a million ways. Specifically, I want to say this: the feminism of my grandmother's generation was loud to combat loud hatred. However, I find my own adolescent battles mainly take place within myself. They are quietly fought. This isn't to say that my life won't become more complicated and extreme as I embark into the working world and find myself in claustrophobic rooms full of men. But the real misogyny I work to offset the most in my day-to-day life is internalized.

For instance, I am always thinking about other people's reactions to me, even when they don't matter that much. I recognize this need to conform and people-please everywhere in women. I saw a video compilation of all of Nikki Haley's self-contradictions yesterday (more than a few) and I thought to myself she's just saying what she thinks they want to hear! I don't agree with most of Nikki Haley's political views, but that desire to ingratiate is embarrassingly familiar to me. I kind of understood it.

On the topic of other people's reactions to who I am, I know my growing body scares my [male?] family members sometimes, because the little baby they knew now has hips and breasts about the same width and size as their wives'. And she wears bikinis, too. I've simultaneously become ashamed and proud of what I look like, when I'm trying and when I'm not. My body frustrates me often because I feel as though it's not something most men have to consider about themselves nearly as much as I do. My body is a political statement, no matter what I do with it. I ask myself cringey questions trying to figure out how I should dress and look: Is it feminist to show some tit? Am I

REALLY doing it for myself? Is it okay if I'm not? I can't say it's not ridiculously confusing. In these situations, I don't know what really can be considered feminist. I don't really think this struggle is new, but I guess my statement certainly highlights this conundrum and its permanence.

Sometimes I wonder about how I would be if I wasn't a woman. I kind of see it reflected in my brother. He actively avoids apologizing. I apologize to inanimate objects for bumping into them. To put things bluntly, he takes up space without concern. I don't wish I wasn't a girl, but I am a world-class ponderer. I ask myself whether, in a different skin, would I be healed from my affliction of eternal irrelevance? And I decide that if I were not contained in this body, I would not worry nearly as much about being loved. I would be happy to be feared. I know that my tangled mind would be worth much more. I knew that even at seven years old.

The unfortunate defense mechanisms we build out of self-hatred from the youngest ages fascinate me, being someone who has definitely engaged in such a performance. Some girls run away as fast as they can from their own femininity to earn acceptance of a male audience. Others find out they get the same twisted acceptance by sexualizing themselves. It then becomes addictive, appealing to this council of men and boys who could decide whether they can treat you as a person or not. You spend years of your life trying to convince them of your valuable qualities.

When I was much younger, if anyone asked me, my favorite color was blue. Not to say girls don't like the color blue, but my favorite colors were actually pink and purple, and I just thought that's what all the other girls would say, and I had decided I was going to set myself apart from them. Blue was my third favorite. I played sports and when I wore dresses (of my own accord), I would announce to everyone that my mom made me wear it. I called myself weird and became obsessed with aliens and making ugly faces in pictures, partially as a misguided attempt to escape this gender role I believed I was too gross to fit. This escape didn't work; I found myself just as unwanted as before. But it's not lost on me the actual thought process of such a phase. I thought defying all things feminine made me different and more interesting. Perhaps better. I wanted to be smart and strong, which I didn't think you could do if you were a girl, no matter how many glittery pink girl power t-shirts from Justice™ my parents and I bought.

My feminist ideas have since evolved of course, and now, since I work in an elementary school after school on Mondays, sometimes I recognize these traits in other little girls. I try to steer them on the right path, but unfortunately, I've found that this conclusion, this self-acceptance of your own girlhood, is something a girl needs to reckon with on her own in order to eventually resent it less. I wish there was more I could be doing for feminism, I truly do. Instead I find myself writing whiny think pieces about how I hate feeling so weak in the eyes of others, how I could maybe one day be strong and command respect, about one day finally feeling comfort in who I am. And maybe that's my own feminism? For myself.

And now, in this year 2024, as I talk about activism and myself, I also need to say that it's no longer just about being a man or a woman anymore. I don't think it ever was. It's about so much more: intersectionality, allyship, offering your support to people who want it. Striving for equality for *everyone* we know, even if that means it's not always about you. I have a lot to be thankful for, but the "unfinishedness" of it all often strikes me. I can obviously speak for myself, but I don't know how to speak for my generation. Maybe I can only say my feminism/activism is an internal battle because I'm still in high school and my world is small. But overall, I think the older generations fought all kinds of these exhausting physical battles so I wouldn't have to. Not to say that my grandmother did not face internalized misogyny, but to underline the point that people just flat out told her she shouldn't do things because she was a woman. We are on different paths here because people don't often just say no to me and calmly explain that it's because I'm a woman, even if it is. They dance around their real issue with me, and the degradation is so subtle I'm left to feel embarrassed and confused with myself.

While what I've just written outlines years more of painstaking work to be done, I'm eternally grateful for the initial feminist waves. When I remember this beautiful transformation we've experienced and the change that is yet to come, I try to love myself just a little bit more, despite everything I've said here. I try to stay motivated to live the life my grandmother made more attainable for me.

Acknowledgments

I WANT TO THANK Meghan, Matthew, Daniel, Abigail, Emily and Nicholas for existing and making my life colorful and challenging. And to Turner, Alexandra, Ava, Ridley, Lucy, Ethan, Rachel, Ryan and Rhys for proving that their parents could be good parents despite their upbringing.

I want to thank my stalwart friend Faith for being there, the team at Sutherland House Books for keeping me going, and, of course, thanks to Trudy Ann.

And I am grateful for my Western Canadian upbringing. As a member of my board of directors once said: "You can take the girl out of Edmonton, but you can't take Edmonton out of the girl."